FOREWORD

When I started this project I never knew I would share so much of myself in my writings. It started as a hobby or a means to get some things out of my head from time to time. While editing this project and preparing it for publishing I had second doubts. I worried myself with the most ridiculous questions. Will people judge me? What about my typos? What will my co-workers think? Will the people that never knew I was a cop look at me differently? The kids that I have interacted with over the years whether it be through my outreach speeches or from coaching read this and think that explains why he was such a lunatic? In the end I decided to commit to the book and omit to my fears. Fears are for failures and I hated the idea of me failing at something because I couldn't commit or over thought the project into submission.

As you read this just know that they are simple thoughts from a simple mind. Yes I have had a few experiences in my life. Some interesting, others sad, but they are my experiences and this is part of my story...enjoy the twisted ride and who knows maybe I'll grow the strength to write volume 2 and share my military memoirs someday.

For the fine folks that I have had an opportunity to work with, that supported this concept and offered encouragement along the way. Thank you and just know that these stories are ours. I made every attempt to articulate these moments in time as accurately as possible with your reflections in my mind during the entire process. The perception of policing is strongly dependent upon the interactions that each of us have with the community every single day and I am proud to say that I feel honored that you have allowed me to serve our community side by side with you.

To my wife and kids I am forever indebted to you. Your patience over the years has been courageous to say the least. The many missed events, overbearing protectiveness, and tolerating my organized chaos and magnetic madness has been a challenge I'm sure. I love you guys, I appreciate you, and your support is my foundation. Thank you!

TABLE OF CONTENTS
MEMOIRS OF A PUBLIC SERVANT

MEMOIRS OF A PUBLIC SERVANT

Memoirs are often written to tell ones story. A series of events actually lived and or experienced by the writer or perhaps the writer has some personal knowledge of the events being presented. At 30 years young I found myself speaking publicly about several of my life experiences and figured why not document them. My public speaking began as a chance encounter at a local underprivileged high school while working in the Community Oriented Policing section (COP). When I worked in COP I would often give presentations on common concerns experienced by realtors, leasing agents, homeowners, neighborhood watch programs, and community organizers. Most of the issues were centered on landlord tenant laws, trespassing, and homelessness. That progressed to high school presentations through a volunteer program at a local high school.

The school fell short by one speaker and sent out a mass email message asking for volunteers to fill in. I choose to speak to a government class that was mostly composed of kids that had either failed the class the year prior or they were struggling to keep up in regular classes for whatever reason. I knew it would be a challenge but I knew that no one else wanted to volunteer and speak to that class. Hence the reason the spot opened up in the first place. After accommodating this one event, I found myself being asked to return several times throughout the year. When they invited me back the second time I was told that the kids requested "the cop". The teacher couldn't believe it.

I had teenage nieces at the time and I knew the right way to speak to young adults in this age range. They didn't need another authoritarian barking orders at them. They wanted to ask questions, real questions and they wanted an adult response. Too many presenters would come to these schools and say the things they thought the kids needed to hear. I took the approach of treating them like young adults. If at their age the decisions they make can permanently affect the rest of their lives, then I wanted to treat them like adults.

Eventually one administrator passed my information to another administrator and before I knew it I was speaking at multiple high schools across the valley. Mostly about my experience growing up in

Los Angeles, graduating and joining the U.S. Army and then becoming a police officer in Las Vegas. Those speeches would always get transformed into a question and answer session with teachers, administrators, and students alike about the proper engagement with law enforcement. As the years progressed the conversations would focus more and more on the things that were being presented in the media. Excessive uses of force, questionable shootings, and other mainstream issues being identified in the media. I was fielding questions from 15 year olds about why unarmed black men were being murdered by the police. When in fact the data showed that more white men were dying at the hands of the police than any other race. I would challenge both the teenagers and the adults in the room to do some research rather than take the media's word for it.

Often times the argument can be made that the data is not accurate because it does not account for the population disparity. There are more white Americans then black Americans. However it would get the rooms engaged in a useful conversation about race relations. The questions wouldn't always be this loaded. Sometimes I fielded the typical teenage questions; "Are you a sneaker head, how much do you make, have you ever shot anyone, why do cops run red lights"? Any question asked I made it a point to answer as straight forward as possible while attempting to put myself in the shoes of the pupil. It wasn't always effective. When all else failed and I had a dry class I would walk them through a call for service using the students as actors during my reenactment. It was like a real life game of Clue, they loved it! The end result would always depend upon the student/ suspect's response to a series of simple questions surrounding search and seizure or other real life scenarios such as Miranda or eyewitness testimony and its reliability.

While journaling or logging my life events I realized that a lot of them were centered on my career as a police officer in Las Vegas Nevada. It's a job like no other in the world, a career that I never imagined, and a lifestyle that I have learned most are curious about but could never imagine doing themselves. The bright lights of a city like Las Vegas can be very inviting. Our city welcomes all and we do this year round. Very few businesses in the tourist corridor close, but there's a city beyond the bright lights. Las Vegas is a city filled with families that work in the service and hospitality industry. We are a city that likes to give you what you want and sometimes more. That service comes at a cost.

I have worked with some of the most loyal and selfless law enforcement professionals in the world. That professionalism and selflessness often comes at a cost. Some pay the ultimate price while serving their community with their lives. Others are surviving while serving. It's a hard job that rarely ends in a happy retirement. Some get out to preserve their sanity and try to salvage marriages and relationships with children. Some folks simply quit and walk away during the training process. Quickly realizing that this profession is not for them. The bold and often unforgiving long termers strive for an opportunity to walk away at the end of an enduring career with hopes of living peacefully in retirement in the quite hills of Montana or Idaho. Perhaps starting over and doing that job that they always wanted.

Sadly this is not the case for a lot of people that make it to the point of retirement. Most (not all) law enforcement retirements are filled with counseling, alcoholism, mending broken relationships, and in not so rare occasions suicide (126 in 2012 of which 18% of those officers suffered from PTSD, and served on average 16 years of service). It's a tough, tough job, an unforgiving career. Yet I couldn't see myself doing anything else. It's as if the career chose me and all of the things I have experienced in my life lead me here.

The broken home I grew up in helps me understand what that defiant adolescent is experiencing. My deployment while serving in the 82nd Airborne division helps me relate to the veteran suffering from PTSD or his poor family that's suffering with him. Growing up in the streets with my cousins in Southern California on food stamps and government assistance allows me to know first-hand what a lot of the low income families are suffering through. Being a husband and a father helps me to communicate with families struggling with domestic dispute concerns. I (as do most officers) make every attempt possible to relate to people while trying to help them solve their problems.

Personal problem solving is probably the largest challenge in my profession. We put so much of ourselves into our work that it begins to eat away at your soul. Taking your work home with you is always a concern. Being able to tuck those worries away inside of your own mind and not let them resurface when you're with your own family and friends is an everlasting concern. Pandora's Box! That's what we call that special place in our own heads. Don't let it over flow or get the best of you. That's the trick to making it through this chosen career.

PART
I

<u>EMPIRICISM BECOMES OFFICER IDIOSYNCRASY</u>

The only source of knowledge is experience
- Albert Einstein

THE HUMAN FACTOR

12-09-2010 Being a police officer / first responder desires you to be a bit more in touch with your feelings then other jobs. By in touch I mean in control of. You must be able to enter a room with a dead baby and treat it like a crime scene, and then moments later look a child molester in the eyes and interview them objectively so as not to effect the case. As a patrol officer your day of emotions can range from captivating highs to maddened lows.

In the police academy we were taught that officers could suffer from what's called hypervigilance. Hypervigilance is basically a system of up's and down's that your body chemistry goes through, throughout the day. Your adrenal glands begin to over produce cortisol. Some officers describe it as sensory overload with a crash or state of exhaustion at the end. Adrenaline and endorphins are being pumped and drained by you all day long. The feeling has been compared to an anxiety attack. Which causes some officers at the end of a 10-hour day to be completely useless. All day long we are making decisions for everyone around us. After all when you dial 911 and the police show up, you expect us to arrive with all of the answers and to solve all of the dilemmas that life has dealt you. In most cases we try to accommodate the communities' request. Unfortunately this can make the easiest of task incredibly difficult for officers once they turn their COP meter off. For example after a day at work and problem solving you go home and your spouse ask you a simple question: what would you like for dinner? The most common COP response is "I don't know whatever you want". Now that officer could have been craving lasagna all day but once they are faced with making that decision they can't. It's not because they are incompetent when not in uniform. It's mostly because the internal well of decision-making has been sucked dry and we need a few hours' sleep to fill the well back up.

Often times we are faced with difficult situations in our lives; the death of a loved one, the bills that are due, or the bad grade that our kid got at school. In that very moment how you deal with it is usually what friends and family remember. No one ever comes to you and says, "Hey I know it was a long day for you, take a nap and get back to me with that solution". You are expected to be the same as everyone else. Your reactions are expected to be just as swift and your responses just as precise as everyone else. No bad days allowed for you Mr./Ms. Officer. No way. Instead the most common response is: What's wrong with you? The reply is usually a subtle…"nothing"!

Well things do bother us and we are effected by our day. In an effort to not allow our friends or family to feel the same way that we do, we shut them out of our work life and try to shelter our personal lives. There is a secret little box buried deep within the brains of every police officer. This mythical little box is filled with all of the crime scenes, burned bodies, slit wrist, dead babies, and malnourished elderly that we deal with. We stuff this box full of junk every day and hope that it never has to surface because my GOD the nightmares that can be scripted out of those tragic pieces of our reality that most people have only seen in fictional horror movies would be farcical.

The call of the day that started my downhill spiral of emotions is one that most people would on the surface say glad that ended that way. One of the Officers at the area command was running vehicle license plates in a mobile home park where stolen vehicles are often dumped. This officer happened to get a return back on a plate that said that the owner of said vehicle was wanted out of California for sex crimes with a minor. After spending sometime with this warrant hit and speaking with the detective in charge in California it was determined that the trailer where this vehicle was parked did indeed belong to said suspect. The detective obviously needed this person taken into custody for further questioning. He explained that the person's computers were to be seized as part of the ongoing investigation.

The Officer requested back up and a knock and talk was conducted. A knock and talk is when officers will knock and if someone answers we have a conversation. Usually when we conduct a knock and talk the person inside the residence opens the door, there is a brief exchange of words, and if the party in question is present they are taken into custody. However on very rare occasions suspects decide to shelter in place and let us know in some not so kind words how they feel about us. Often times you can hear the person stacking furniture, smashing things inside of the house, or shouting threats our way. We call these situations barricades. This particular suspect decided that he didn't want to play nice today and barricaded himself inside of his trailer. He then saw it fit to show the officers outside through the window that he had a firearm of some sort. A rifle of unknown make, model, or caliber.

This has now become a situation where because of the location and the infrastructure of the surrounding mobile homes, where we must evacuate roughly 60 to 70 people from their homes. When evacuating folks you have to consider several things to including accommodating those with special needs such as medications that need to be refrigerated, young children that need to be entertained, and of course the occasional person that decides they're not leaving their home because their asshole neighbor is having a bad day. While all of that is sorted out by the valiant efforts of approximately 10 to 15 police officers, you are simultaneously dealing with the person in question. If you are lucky enough to have a negotiator in your area then great, if not then you do the best you can with what you have until a negotiator can arrive. Meanwhile the boys in the green PJ's (SWAT) officers or operators depending on who you are speaking to, are gearing up and getting ready to do what they do best. Persuade the unwilling, make a tactical entry, or possibly blow some stuff up!

After about 4 hours of trying to coach the guy on the inside to come join the party on the outside then cool stuff starts to happen. BOOM, BOOM, BANG-BOOM. Flash bangs are thrown and the subject is asked to step outside or we will go inside and remove you. After a few minutes of not getting a response most of us that have been on several of these capers know that one of two things must have occurred by now. Either the subject has decided not to comply and is not exiting the residence because he wants the special attention from SWAT, or he has killed himself.

That is correct folks you guessed it, this time the guy that was wanted for child sex crimes who possibly has more child pornography on his personal computer has decided to kill himself. Only this guy didn't use a gun or take pills to do the dirty deed. No way. This guy decided to stab himself in both sides of his neck, his stomach, slit his wrist and bleed out on his bed. Sounds unbelievable right! Well that's exactly what happened. Rather than face the court system and deal with the crimes that you have been alleged to have committed, you kill yourself in one of the most brutal and barbaric ways I have ever seen. Judging by the amount of blood on the bed it's safe to say that this guy has been dead for at least an hour if not more. Which means that everyone has been evacuating, pulling security, and focusing solely on you for no reason.

Now we are stuck with no closure for the families of the victims, the apologizing for the inconvenience caused to the neighbors, and of course a messy clean up. Thousands of dollars gone and so is the source of so much agony. It's all kind of bitter sweet in some weird ironic way.

After dealing with this kind of a call at work my wife and I drove to her Uncles house when I got off of work. Her uncle has recently been placed on hospice due to him growing sicker after a long battle back and forth with cancer. Uncle looked bad today. His blue eyes pierced right through me as I sat next to his hospital bed. His pupils looked like pin drops and it almost seemed as if he was looking through me and not at me. I felt like I was living the old saying, "the eyes are the key to the soul". He was definitely out of it.

Despite his level of consciousness he knew we were there. He responded to most of what we were saying in typical Uncle Fashion. Using his favorite key phrases, hey asshole, and fuck you. I couldn't help but to smile at him and think that if this really is it, he was going out his way. Being the same asshole that everyone loved to hate. He insisted on drinking a Budweiser from a glass cup. With every sip that hit his lips you could almost feel the pressures of life falling off of his shoulders. I secretly thought to myself, man this family isn't ready for this. I wanted to do something, anything to try to ease the distress and the burden but what could I do. After the day that I had just experienced I was useless. We knew things were bad and all I found myself doing was sitting there being a buffer of some sort.

PERSONAL LOSS

12-11-2010

This morning at approximately 0130HRS my wife's Uncle passed away in his home after a long fight with cancer. While my wife and kids were at her uncle's house I was working overtime at Caesars Palace. My wife called me immediately and let me know what happened. I instantly felt saddened by the news but at the same time I was a bit relieved for him.

Just one-day prior we were visiting him at home and he was displaying some obvious signs that his time was shortening. He kept muttering random things about going on a trip with his dad and going fishing. He also stated that he wanted to get out of the bed and go home. At one point we sat him up at his request and he realized that he was at his house he asked to be laid back down. When I sat next to him he apologized to me because he kept saying that he wanted to go home.

Uncle: I'm sorry I keep saying I want to go home; I already am at home…shit!

Me: As I held his hand, "no worries Unc we know what you mean. It's all-good".

The vibe around the house was definitely eerie. None of his grand kids could understand why their grandpa was getting so upset with them over small things. His daughter was drinking away the pain. My wife sat on the couch and held a conversation with his wife and one of his other daughters. They asked my wife all the tough questions that no one wants' to know the answers too. You see on 12-31-2008 we unfortunately lost my wife's mom at home to cancer, and then on 04-12-2009 we lost her father to congestive heart failure AKA a broken heart after his wife's passing. I am of the belief that our unfortunate experiences and how we handled them caused everyone to believe that we are the rocks of the family, the strong ones to call on in troubling times.

When I finally got off I went home and changed out of my uniform immediately and was headed out the door to be with my wife and kids. Just as I was leaving the house my wife was pulling into the driveway. She looked exhausted. My wife asked me if I could drive her to her friend's house so she could take her final for her last remaining class of the semester. You see my wife is in nursing school. After taking care of both of her parents while they were on hospice she knew her calling was to help those in need. Great timing, right? Obviously I agreed and drove her.

As we drove to her friend's house she explained the night's chain of events to me. I just sat there silently and tried to absorb as much of it as possible. Was it going to resolve anything? Nope not at all, but sometimes we just need someone to listen. Not try to problem solve or even offer to help fix anything-just listen. At this point in our lives we have experienced a lot of personal loss. Mostly while in our early adult years.

My grandmother passed away right after I graduated basic training. To this day I believe she waited for me to complete that phase of training because she knew I wouldn't be able to handle her passing while dealing with the chaos of Basic Training. I was at my advanced training still going through the in-processing steps at my new company when our company commander entered the room and called me into his office. As strange as this seemed I was still a brand new private in the Army and had no idea what this could be about. He sat me down and said you have a Red Cross message. At the time I had no idea what a Red Cross message was or what any of that meant. If a family emergency occurs and you need to get that message sent to a service member your best course of action is to contact the Red Cross and give them any of the service member's information that you may have. Name, social security number, possible installation, anything. They will see to it that the message is delivered as promptly as possible.

September 16th 2001 I lost the most important person in my life. One year later to the date my son was born and I gained that missing soul back and started to feel complete again. Life has that kind of weird way of coming back at you full circle. My grandmother raised me most of my life and had a huge influence on the person that I became. She didn't have much but would give everything she had to anyone that was in need. She was extremely tough on me, never allowing me to accept defeat or loose a fight. "Go back and do it again! You're better than that, you're a man and men don't let themselves get beat".

Wilma Stiles was a wonderful soul who loved all things Christ, would burn holy candles, read scripture aloud, attend any church within a 1 mile radius, and had me baptized 4 times by my teenage years. She smoked heavily, drank rarely, and loved the hell out of people. She would cook up a storm with the little money that we had just so we would have extras for anyone that stopped by. Thanksgiving was always a feast on a fixed income by any means necessary. I can recall picking up food from church pantries, and hitting up the local food market with our government distributed food stamps. We had nothing but I always felt like we had everything that we needed.

When I met my wife in high school I was no longer living with my grandmother she had gotten ill and moved back to Kentucky to be closer to her family. My aunt took me in for a while which allowed me to stay in California. We lived in Inglewood for a while, Gardena for a bit, and a few other less desirable locations. She worked hard but there were six of us and that situation was complicated. After meeting my wife and being introduced to her family her parents took to me and welcomed me into their lives with open arms. Me, that ghetto little street rat! It was a shocking experience and one that changed the landscape of my existence and added a chapter to my life that truly shaped and molded much of my adult life.

Gloria Jean Murray (Jeannie as we called her) my wife's mother was the most compassionate person I had ever met in my life. She reminded me of my grandmother in that sense. Everyone was welcome into her home until you crossed the line. She loved animals and would rescue every stray dog she came across, a trait that my wife inherited. She showed me a side of the human heart that I never knew existed. Total and unconditional love! Loving with your heart not your head.

Regardless of whether or not a situation surrounding a person was their own fault or would bring any drama along with them. She would welcome them with open arms. This woman collected cans and would place them on her porch for a homeless gentlemen to come by and collect on a regular bases. She fed him from time to time and it was just a normal part of her routine. Between raising her daughter (my future wife) and half of the neighborhood street kids, nursing ill animals back to health, and working insane hours, she always managed to take the time to prepare a nice meal for anyone that wanted to stop by.

Jeannie getting diagnosed with cancer years later subdued my soul. How in the hell could someone so caring be cursed with such an illness? After the doctors opened her up and realized she was inoperable that news was devastating. This woman was our Mother Theresa. She had extended her hand to the world and offered every ounce of her goodness to help any and every one that she could. Her home was often a temporary dwelling for those in transition, a make shift hospital for those recovering, and always a warm and inviting place to get a meal in you before hitting the road. Jeannie's passing still doesn't make much sense to me. A person like that should live forever. Instead she was taken from us all far too early meanwhile the world's miscreants get to roam the earth wreaking havoc and victimizing folks.

John Murray, Jeannie's husband, and my wife's father was another unique soul. This man owned more cars' at one time then I will probably own in a lifetime. He wasn't always as welcoming as Jeannie but he knew when to push and when to just let her do her thing. If she ever offered him up to help someone he would cuss up a storm, grab his tools, and head on out.

John was a fabulous man that loved his gold jewelry and cologne. Those were always a guarantee for him for Christmas. He had about 50 fragrances and each served a purpose. He taught me the art of looking good and the reason why image was important. People will judge you without realizing they are judging you. Give them something to judge you by! John was a southern man with a laugh and a smile that would warm any room. But if you pissed him off he let you know it. John wore his emotions on his sleeves and he would tell you if you did something that he didn't agree with. He never held a grudge and was quick to forget.

Standing at 6 feet and maybe 4 inches he had a commanding presence about him. If you were ever blessed to be out with John you never paid for anything. That was his gift. He always had a way of making it all work. Big John would tease the hell out of you with his classic "I forgot my wallet line", but he always insisted on covering the tab. The man simply enjoyed taking care of others in his grumpy own way. He had his convictions and his absolutes and no one was changing his mind. Driving nice cars, and keeping them perfectly polished was all a part of the image. I swear every piece of his clothing was dry cleaned with heavy starch. He always shined and made everyone else that he was with feel just as bright as he has. It was a magnificent talent that I wish I could duplicate. My kiddos are a lot like him in many ways. If you're on their good side they want to give you the world. But piss them off and you will know it.

John's passing hurt no more or less then the passing of Jeannie. My wife and I learned so much from each of them and when their energy was taken from us I felt an instant need to do better. A need to continue to be the good that they were in this world. I know that I can never fill their shoes and never intended to try to replace them. However I will always strive to fill the void that was left with their passing. When I'm doing my job as a law enforcement officer I often think about them. I don't waste time wondering if they would be proud, rather I wonder if they would agree with my decision-making, candor, and stern yet flexible levels of compassion.

FAMILY IRONY

07/04/2012 If there was ever a story that helped you understand the meaning of the word IRONY this was it. While working in a plain-clothes capacity I was patrolling to the area of 5600 Boulder Hwy, which is A Local Weekly Hotel. It's one of the lowest income areas we have in our entire city. Violent crime is rampant and the frequency of narcotics related crimes such as prostitution, theft, and even murder is higher than most low-income communities in other large cities. Working in plain-clothes means that officers are dressed in regular street clothes. It's not quite undercover operations but it is similar. An undercover operation requires much more training, years of experience, and a lot more resources.

We had a few deals lined up to purchase some stolen property from a guy on craigslist. When doing this kind of work, you have to project things and we tend to make it a habit to announce to one another, the subjects that we plan to "run on". Running on a subject means that you will be interacting with them. That can be purchasing narcotics, stolen merchandise, or setting up future deals. It's dangerous work but can be exciting and extremely rewarding. Returning someone stolen property has always been one of my favorite things to do as an officer.

Off in the distance at approximately 500 meters from me I can see a black male adult walking in my direction with two black female adults. I think to myself, "those look like a good set of potential clients to set something up with for later". One of my partners calls my cell phone and basically says the same thing. He describes them to me and says they will be there momentarily. Black male 6 feet, sagging pants, wearing a wave cap. It sounded like he was describing me for a second, but I knew the subject because I could see him clearly walking in my direction. The two chicks that he's with look like a couple of prostitutes my partner says.

As the male approaches me I realize that I know him. Not in a law enforcement kind of way. I tried to quickly turn away but it was too late, he greets me with a hug and a smile. "What's good cuzzo, it's been a minute since I seen you". The male states. "Oh shit man what you doin out here", I reply. We exchange a series of words then he continues to walk away with his lady friends. The girls both have

31

over sized hooped earrings in their ears, one is wearing really tight jeans and Jordan's, and the other is wearing a mini skirt that's extra mini and some nasty worn out Adidas. Neither of them speak to me they just stare. Thank God, that buys me some time.

I called my supervisor and let him know that the "good target" that I know we were all watching is my cousin. Not a play cousin, not a guy that I know from around the way. But my real family. My boss says, "okay Charlie I understand, it's between you and me. No one needs to know". I say, "Thanks Frankie I appreciate that". My cousin then exits the store with his lady friends and comes back to me ready to engage in more small talk. I kindly pull him to the side and say "bro can you do me a favor and leave this area". He looks at me with a puzzled stare. You see I don't tell very many people what it is that I do for a living, and this is the reason why. I say it again…"you should leave bro". I then ask him for his number and say "I'll call you later and explain".

For me this is a really personal moment in my life. This is a guy that had the same fate as me. We grew up together, lived under the same roof and broke bread together. Now here we are on two complete opposite sides of the life and the law. It's safe to assume that if he was cruising these streets with those girls he was into the shady lifestyle that was prevalent in this area.

This haunted me for a while. What the hell was the difference between my life and his? Why am I working for the police department and my own cousin is creeping around a shit part of town with the less desirables? Apart of me wanted to quit the job and not have to worry about stuff like this ever again. A drastic overreaction, but nonetheless a thought that crept through my mind. "Naw, that's not the answer"! I thought maybe if I reach out to him and offer him a place to stay and an opportunity to change, maybe he just hasn't had that chance yet. I dial the number a few days later and his prepaid phone is no longer working. I go back to the neighborhood a few times looking for my cousin but no luck. That still bothers me to this day.

Lil Jay I pray that you're ok and I think about you and everything that your pops did for me growing up. We grew up living in a small

2-bedroom apartment in Gardena California riding our bikes all over the place causing all kinds of trouble, nothing criminal, just mischievous. He was a few years younger than me, but he had an older brother that sometimes lived with us and sometimes lived with his mom. It wasn't the worst life but by no means was it pleasant.

We saw all kinds of stuff coming up in that old neighborhood. Crack was a huge thing in that area at the time. I still remember someone stealing all of our stuff while we were moving into our apartment. We dropped a load off in our U-Haul and went back for another. When we returned everything was gone but our clothes. They stole TV's, some furniture, and any little thing they could exchange for dope. My uncle (his dad) went walking around and found the neighborhood dope man. He asked about our stuff but there was a street code that wasn't about to be broken on our behalf. We assumed our new apartment was one of the old dope spots. On a few occasions during random hours we had crack heads knocking on the door asking for D-block. My uncle would run them off and tell us all to go back to bed. It's easy for me to laugh about it now, but at the time it was frustrating. You felt powerless and, like predators surrounded you, waiting for you to slip up and leave something unsecure. I had a bike or two stolen from that neighborhood. Maybe that's why we kept ourselves busy by running the streets and playing in the alleys on old mattresses and behind abandoned buildings on mounds of dirt. It cleared your head and made you forget about your circumstances.

JUST A NOTE

8/3/2012

I'm headed back to Reno for drill. This weekend we will be conducting range operations. That should be a good time; it's not the training that gets me all worked up, but rather the flight. I refuse to fly in uniform because I don't want people thanking me for my service. I serve my country for myself and my own personal desires. Not to appease the masses or receive recognition. Sure, people are just trying to express their appreciation and they mean well. But I always feel awkward.

It makes it really difficult because everyone that I travel with fly's in uniform and all these great Americans walk up and shake their hands looking them in the eyes and say thank you very much for your service. This may be a bit weird of me but I don't like that. I kind of miss the pre 911 days when soldiers served honorably with little to no recognition, and walked through airports as a distant unknown.

Don't get me wrong I love the patriotism but the lack of acknowledgement was just fine for me. Plus I feel like a security threat when I'm in uniform. Rather than being a big shiny target for some slimy terrorist I'd rather be the unsuspecting guy that comes out of nowhere on the plane and causes dude some damage. I make it a point to wear nothing that resembles a soldier. I sit away from the other soldiers and try to look every person in the eyes when I walk past them. I want to feel their good or bad vibes. Yes it's extreme and probably a little bit crazy to think that I would actually make a difference in an emergency situation. However I certainly have mentally prepared myself for the possibility of shenanigans occurring. I guess that's just the post 9-11 world we're living in.

05-14-2014 From time to time we get the luxury of changing up our type of patrol. It depends on your supervisor, department needs, equipment available, and some other non-important factors. What makes variable patrolling fun or interesting is who you are partnered with. A few years back while working an overtime event I met my present day partner Rob Angel.

I have to take a moment to introduce you to Rob's personality. That thing deserves a book of its own. Rob is my age and grew up in similar circles in Southern California. He's an animated dude who aggressively talks with his hands. He loves telling stories, and his stories are fanFREAKINGtastic. This dude can act out the smallest scene and turn it into a Shakespearean drama. Here's a few other really pertinent facts that will help you better understand my partner Rob. He's been married multiple times, has a few kids by multiple women, has been disciplined by the department on numerous occasions for on duty shenanigans; he enjoys his bars and drinks in multiple rounds, oh and of course he's a diehard Dodger's fan and hates the Raiders. Rob is extremely outgoing and insists on being heard in every room that he enters. He's not loud in an obnoxious kind of way; instead he creates a curious demeanor that draws people towards him.

We have worked together in various capacities and the guy has managed to adjust to every situation in an almost seamless fashion. Rob is an east L.A., legitimate street cat who like me can't figure out how we ever got this job. It's not that we aren't qualified; it's just that kids that grow up in our neighborhoods don't typically grow up and work in law enforcement. Here's where all of this ties into play.

I can recall an incident that Rob and I responded to. We were circling the station at the end of our day and overheard a domestic violence call that stated that the victims' brother, believed to be under the influence of narcotics was aggressively swinging and striking family members with a hammer. The details further stated that the male had fled the scene in an unknown direction of travel. As we're responding Rob and I are discussing our approach if we run into this guy. I'll be contact and talk and Rob would be cover and watch my back. As we get closer to the residence Rob suggests that we turn right at the next street, I oblige. Bam! Our bad guy is right there in the middle of the street. I stop about 40 or so yards back and jump out of my patrol car and begin to give him verbal commands.

Me: Yo my man come here! (In my stern, I'm the police voice)

Bad Guy: turns and faces me, doesn't say a word and just rushes towards me.

I can see the hammer in his hand but he isn't swinging it or anything. I deploy my Taser just as a cautionary tool, in case he doesn't stop. By the time I get my Taser drawn and aimed at the angry hammer guy he's about 5 feet away from me. All of a sudden Rob hits this guy with the cleanest form tackle I have ever seen by a guy in uniform.

Rob: Looks up at me…"you ok Baby boy".

Me: Places handcuffs on bad guy and calls for medical. He scratched his arm during the little scuffle and was bleeding everywhere. Not to mention the spitting.

Rob tackles this guy and then looks up at me as if we were in a movie and just says… "You ok Baby boy". We still laugh about that one to this day. Rob says, "You know that's my movie", referring to the 2001 movie Baby Boy starring Tyrese. In the end I was more upset about the paperwork I now had to do at the end of my shift because of a Taser that didn't even work. He had on a few shirts and the prongs never engaged his skin. We could have driven to the station since it was the end of our shift and ignored the call, but that's not how we roll.

This is the thing about Rob that impresses me the most. A few weeks later we are selected to do bike patrol in an apartment complex that's been active with burglaries. While we're pedaling around we find a small school on the outskirts of our assigned area. We figured lets go check it out and maybe find a clean spot to use the bathroom. After we are buzzed into the school, the lady working the front counter nervously ask why we're here. "Recess and chocolate milk"! Shouts

Rob. The lady just stares in total confusion. I follow up with

"bathroom if that's ok". She opens up the back door and points us

across the courtyard. Just as we start to make our way towards the

restroom a group of special needs children and their teachers aid are

exiting their bungalow and heading towards the open fields. I use the

restroom and when I come back out Rob in fully engaged in a game

of kickball with some of the kids. I join him and we play for at least

a good half an hour and then the teacher says they have to go. The

kids can't be out that long; Las Vegas heat can be brutal at this time

of year. The kids are so happy; they hug us as they walk back inside.

We leave and head back to our bike patrol duty.

For the next several weeks that we were assigned to bike patrol we

made it a point to go back to that school at the same time every day

(unless we were on a call) and play a little kickball. It got to the

point that the front counter lady wouldn't even ask anymore. When

she saw us she just buzzed us in and we played with the kids.

The teachers' aides loved us for helping take a little pressure off of them. There were way more special needs kids then they could handle alone. During one of our last visits to the school we arrived late and the kids were all at lunch. We asked if we could join them. As we walked into the cafeteria standing tall in our police uniforms an awkward silence fail over the cafeteria. Rob shouts out, "where's the chocolate milk"! We walk around speak to a few kids, and make it a point to hang out with the tables that are less popular. The kids loved every minute of it, and the teachers managing this feeding time madness gave us an open invitation to come back anytime because the kids were so well behaved when we were around. My man Rob Angel was quick to intervene and even quicker to care, despite his East L.A. swagger and I could careless attitude towards policy and politics. Maybe that's what makes him such a great cop. He polices for the people, not the pressures put on you by the department.

EMPTY BOTTLES

04-16-2015 Alcohol has been called many things. It has been seen as a drug, a sleep aide, a recreational choice for adults, and a truth serum. The act of drinking alcohol is not necessarily a bad thing however like most other vices, if you're not careful it can bite you in the ass. I woke up this morning to a kitchen with approximately 25 empty bottles. Now before you go crazy and start thinking that I tried to kill myself with a bottle of Jack Daniels let me explain the situation.

Last night I started drinking, one glass of whiskey neat here and there. In the comfort of my own home and on a full stomach. Not a big deal at all. Until I hit the bottom of a bottle of Jim Beam and started expressing my feelings about everything under the sun. I drunk texted several members of my family and expressed my true feelings about years of absence from my father. I texted several co-workers (including my boss) and who knows who else. According to my wife I began to talk about suicide and punched my headboard multiple times after knocking pictures off of the walls. Needless to say I became a sloppy drunk.

Now is where I explain the suicide stuff. No I do not want to hurt myself at all…however a co-worker, a fellow Officer killed himself with his department issued rifle about a week ago. Then I received a message from another one of my friends that his father just committed suicide. I usually don't share my feelings or discuss these types of things with anyone. I tuck them away deep into my head and forget about them. Mr. Jim Beam weakened my defenses and everything came out all at once. I just exploded with emotion; anger, fear, sadness, love, everything all at once. A very dangerous cocktail for a dude my size!

Back to the empty bottles! Apparently my wife got so upset over the whole thing that she dumped every single bit of alcohol out and left the bottles on the bar and kitchen counter for me to clean up the next morning. It was a heart breaking scene, tequila, gin, rum, and whiskey all gone. Down the black hole, into no man's land called the sink. As I toss one bottle at a time into the trash I felt little bitty whiskey burps coming back up. I was kind of hurting, which is unusual for me. Normally I can pound a bottle and wake up the next day with no side effects, no hangover, and unfortunately no knowledge of what happened the night before. I wouldn't say I have an issue. It's not exactly a normal thing for me. I just have some kind of herculean trigger that allows me to blackout and wake up totally refreshed with nothing on my mind.

Well that's all over with for a while at least. The well has run dry and the Gin is no longer an option, nor the Vodka, nor the occasional shot of Tequila to help me forget about the blood I saw that day at work. The "small" glass of Moscato with dinner to help ease away the thought of the beaten child or abused mother are gone for now. The Margarita madness to wash away the complaints and the filth I deal with daily both from the Police department and Military. It's a hard ass life and it has aged me years beyond belief. I try to fight the urge and use other outlets such as physical training or typing this memoir. However sometimes a nice chilled glass of Whiskey neat just does the trick and it hits a lot faster.

Like I mentioned earlier I usually wake up feeling totally refreshed with no memory. I haven't quite figured out if that's a good or a bad thing.

This chapter has been pinging around in my mind's eye for quite some time. Keep or delete? Judgment and resentment! Will people read this and instantly think they have me figured out. He's an alcoholic and all cops are drunks! None of that is true. However I know that perception is reality and I can see people perceiving me as something that I'm not based on words typed onto a page. Honestly I could care less about people judging me and developing their opinions of me based on some words in a book. I do however care about the reputation of those in my profession(s). Soldiers and law enforcement folks execute grueling task, see some of the world's worst, and experience situations that are unimaginable. I love every minute of it, even the horrible things make you a more seasoned person and that experience may be hard at the moment but that hardened freeze frame in time may benefit someone else later on down the road.

ANOTHER YEAR

05-05-2015 If the good lord blesses me with breath in my lungs in the morning I'll be 32 years old.... that's 11 years older than I ever imagined when I was a kid. That's 11 years of gifted bliss from the maker himself. You see when I was kid growing up in shit neighborhoods I would pray that I could make it to at least 21. I feel like anything after that has been borrowed time. Life has been good and I have been the recipient of many blessings. I am thankful for each of them, as I am equally thankful for my challenges. As they have all made me the man that I am today collectively. I can only hope to receive many more years of experiences. Experiences that may not have always been positive, but they have been mine. I own them; they are my stories to tell, my visions to store, my truths to unfold, and my miseries to despise. I own them all, good, bad and indifferent.

Today I did my traditional one-year-older PT session. One of the things that I have adopted on my birthday is a special workout regimen. I try to get this done every year either on my actual birthday or the day before or after. It just depends on my schedule (I rarely take the day off of work). The regiment is really simple. Birthday sets and birthday reps. I'll try to do another one tomorrow but I figured why wait until tomorrow, to do what can be done today. Last year it was 10 reps of 31 sets of various exercises. I chose 31 sets because it was my 31st birthday. This year I intended on running 3.2 miles with a Rucksack and then doing my 333-pushup challenge plus 32 more push-ups. I ended up running just over 5 miles and did A LOT of pushups. So I guess my theme PT will have to wait.

5-6-2016 33 years young!!! Today I turned 33 and I actually feel pretty good. I just had a physical at work and everything was picture perfect. Not the norm for men with my chosen professions. Usually soldiers and police officers start to fall apart after about 10 years on the job. I contribute my continued youthfulness to my busy lifestyle. I think that staying active both mentally and physically have really helped me in a major way. I keep my mind busy and refuse to have a moment of rest that last longer than a few hours. The one thing that I wish I could figure out is my sleeping habits. I mean of course I could eat better, but I particularly enjoy the freedom of having a piece of red meat or cheddar on a burger from time to time. Plus dessert is my favorite meal. Nonetheless, other than sleep I maintain a fairly decent lifestyle. Maintaining a positive outlook on things is important to me, which is extremely hard to do when you see terrible people do terrible things for a living.

I turned 33 so I will knockout 33 sets of 33 reps. I usually choose one particular exercise and just grind it out. It's a way for me to tell myself that I am still young and energetic. This year I chose to do bicep curls. The weight totally depends on how I am feeling. It's a pretty simple concept. It's just one of those things that keeps me young in my own mind. After all a youthful mind produces a youthful body and soul.

I never have been the type to plan stuff for my birthday. I don't care about going to concerts or catching shows or whatever else people tend to do on their special day. For me the gift of life is usually enough. The fact that I was blessed with another year is reason enough to celebrate. This year however was not like other years, my birthday fell during one of my regular scheduled days off, and my wife happen to be off. She surprised me with a few things that clearly I would never setup for myself.

She took me to her nail lady and got me, what I like to call a feetacure... more commonly known as a pedicure. Fellas, you gotta try this! It's basically a foot massage with oranges, some magic honey mix, and some other secret woman type potion that made me feel like I was walking on clouds afterwards. Now before you go being all judgy on me please understand that this is not a normal activity for me AT ALL. We ate breakfast at one of my favorite local spots. Then she had a deep tissue massage setup for me at one of the SPA's at a casino, which was phenomenal, absolutely incredible.

It was like a full body reset. I usually think that I feel ok after training and working out, but nope, not the case. Your body doesn't know what a reset is until you have a deep tissue massage. I felt light headed after I stood up, but relaxed like no other. Later on that evening we met up with some of her co-workers and did the drinks thing at a steak house. Then we left there and went downtown to first Friday. First Friday is an artsy type event that is held in the art district in downtown Las Vegas. Not the type of place you would expect a guy like me to enjoy, but I have wanted to go down there and check it out. It did not disappoint, I enjoyed the people watching, but more importantly I enjoyed the art. There is definitely an eclectic display of art and music down there. Dare I use the words beautiful chaos. The only thing I walked away with was a giant jar of fresh local honey. But I still enjoyed the venue. I wasn't prepared to purchase any art pieces that evening. Maybe next time!

PARENTAL? GUIDANCE

I will NEVER forget these words "CHARLESTON WHO". My sister called me one day out of the blue and informed me that the guy who helped create me was in the hospital. She proceeded to catch me up on his health concerns, relationship status and some other meaningless nonsense about the dude. I listened because I have always been curious and I always had the thought in the back of my mind that maybe he would want to meet his grandkids (who I like to think are pretty freaking awesome). She gives me the number to the hospital and says he's probably there alone away from his girlfriend so maybe if you call he will speak to you. I sat on the number for hours over thinking every possible conversation that we may have. You see, I have no memory of ever spending time with this man; I have no photos with him outside of a blurry 1-year-old birthday party. I've always been told that my parents got divorced when I was around two years old.

I finally grew the courage to call. It's unbelievable but my heart still races when I think about it, in fact my eyes are filled with tears as I'm typing this. Yes it still pisses me off!

Me: Hello is this _____

Him: yeah who is this

Me: it's Charleston

Awkward silence falls over the phone for what felt like a lifetime but was probably only a few seconds

Me: Charleston Hartfield your son. You and _____ had me back in 83.

Him: Charleston who...

That WHO echoed in my head like a loudspeaker down a cave.

Me: (Instant Rage) Charleston your son...How many Charleston's do you know, you gave me that stupid name... you know what never mind I messed up and dialed the wrong dude. My bad man.... click! I sat there and cried for probably a solid 15 minutes and then kindly reminded myself that I was fine 20 minutes ago and that I would be fine 20 minutes from now. After all what did you really expect from an intentionally absent figure after 30 years. That phone call was life changing. It hurt in a special kind of way. I feel like it hurt more because I didn't expect for it to hurt. I got sucker punched with a double downed dose of reality. He didn't want to be a father, why would I think he actually wanted to be a grandfather.

I called my sister after I settled myself and explained to her what happened. She apologized even though she didn't need to. She then explained that she was going to call and speak to him...I told her not to bother with it.

Over the next few hours I received messages from my other half siblings expressing their hatred for him. None of it mattered to me. I wrote it off as another life lesson, don't go kicking over rocks that sit on top of an anthill, the result might be devastating. This guy has a Preacher, a Doctor, a psychology graduate that's a certified life coach, and Me as his children and he still cant accept us and his own. Total madness and personally I have no time for shenanigans like that. Made it this far without you in my world and I guess now I have even more motivation to make it further. Not going to lie that one minute phone call cut me deep but its another wound that'll be packed deep and the scar will never be explained to those that ask. Ill add that one to my therapy list.

11-25-2015 Today I received a call from my sister. She informed me that our "father" had passed away. She believed in his sleep, but it was unconfirmed initially. I was at a loss for words and my emotions were instantly tangled. I felt relieved, yet sad. I felt angry and even more betrayed then before. When she called me I was at work and didn't know how to respond. This may sound pathetic, but as soon as I got into my car at the end of my workday I cried. Only it wasn't a sad, sorrow driven cry. It was more of an angered cry of frustration. I mean surely he knew he was sick. I understand fully that no one knows the exact time of his or her death, but he could have reached out.

He could have called and at least acknowledged me, that's all I wanted from the man before he left this earth was acknowledgment that I exist. I just wanted to know that he really did know who I was.

That I was doing everything in my power to not be HIM. In the end his sick fatherless avoidance wins again. Even though he just passed away and in my mind I feel obligated to be upset. I cannot find it in myself to become emotional. It's a really sad and disturbing feeling.

11-26-2015 Last night my son was at a local pizza spot with his teammates. My wife asked me to join them there after taking our daughter to dance. Against my better judgment I went. The entire time I felt distant and out of place. Maybe the universe was sending me his energy, letting me know that it was time. Maybe I was just tired, I don't know. Either way he's still gone or I will never know what I meant to him if anything at all. Here's why I shared this piece of information. The absence of this man has partially shaped who I am today. Good, bad, or indifferent I am who and what I am because of his absence. I was given all of the information for the funeral and for half a second I thought about attending. NAW Fuck that! This may sound super petty, but how can I sacrifice the time, money, and effort to attend the funeral of a man who claimed to not know my name. "CHARLESTON WHO"

3-12-2016 Taking a leap of faith is challenging, but sometimes you have to pray and just take a chance. I have had a broken relationship with my mother for quite sometime. She called me out of the blue a few months back and asked if she could come out to Las Vegas for a few weeks and hangout. I was hesitant about welcoming her back into my life and especially into my home. She has never been to my house and my kids don't really know her. My son has seen her once before several years ago. But she hasn't exactly been the model grandmother. I explained to her that she had to have a 2-way ticket with a definitive return date. No bullshit, and no surprises. I was definitely stern about it and probably a little bit aggressive. However I felt an obligation to be protective of my wife and kids against a stranger with biological ties.

The strain in the relationship that I have with my mother is evident. It's something that still causes me great anguish, even at 32 years old. I tried to be more understanding of her situation but after her visit I felt even more frustrated. I get it, expecting perfection is just ridiculous, but man she is rough around the edges and just hard to deal with. For years I have tried to simply get the truth from her about my childhood to no avail. I have given up on that idea. In an effort to be a better person I told her that she could be a grandmother to my kids and to try to focus her efforts on that relationship.

My son made it obvious that he does not like her. He was the typical teenage boy and kind of distant which was ok at first. However I found him taking it a step further from time to time by making fun of her and repeating the things that she would say in a less then respectful manner. My wife quickly pointed out the fact that his treatment of her was based upon my example. I was confusing him. I allowed a stranger to enter his life that was pretending to know everything about him, about us. It was very difficult.

My daughter on the other hand acted as if my mother was her personal play date. She thought she was the funniest thing around and laughed up a storm at everything she said. God bless her naivety. I wish I could erase all of the memories and just start over and try to appreciate her for who she is. The problem is that the longer she stayed the more I realized that I don't like who she is. In fact I found myself counting down the days until her departure. From time to time she would share some worthless story about my childhood and I would beg her to stop. It all seemed made up to me. I hated every minute of it. She would attempt to explain my ancestry and family history and nothing seemed real or authentic. I almost felt like I was living through a Quentin Tarentino movie with one of those twisted ass plots. I begged her to stop, please don't share any more stories. Then it happened, she began to explain how much my father loved me and why she divorced him. Mind you I never knew any of this. I lost it! I reacted with total disgust and told her to fucking stop. Don't ever bring him up again in my house. I was over it, and have managed to cope with his nonexistence for 32 years. The last thing I needed was her input causing me any emotional distress. You can choose to remember him however you wish, but not knowing him has been a common thing for me. Let's just leave it at that.

We moved on from that conversation and she proceeded to tell me all about how she tried to give me 5 names when I was born instead of the 4 that I currently have. The lovely folks at Kaiser Permanente Hospital kindly informed her that all of that wouldn't fit on one birth certificate. While she was present at my house she made it a point to call me by all 5 names on a regular bases. I was annoyed, but my wife and kids found it entertaining. She wanted me to have the name of all of the great men from our family, grandfathers, great grandfathers and such. It's a noble concept, but not with 5 different names, that's just excessive.

Maybe now is as good a time as any to discuss my "relationship" with my mother. You see I don't have very many memories from my childhood. The few that I do have are mostly small pockets of me living with her for brief stints in between living with my grandmother in various parts of southern California. I moved a lot growing up. I attended maybe 7 or 8 different schools before I made it to high school and decided that it was best for me to do my own thing and then met my wife and her family who basically took in a street rat. I digress... My guess is that she lived a lifestyle that probably wasn't indicative of raising a young boy...especially in L.A. in the late 80's and 90's. I'm perfectly ok with that, and can excuse her absence based on situational circumstances.

My issue is that 30 years later I still can't get her to just tell me the truth and to admit that she was absent. Forget absent how about apologizing for letting me live through the abusive relationships she had with many come and go boyfriends over the years. As I matured and realized just how bad it was I began to resent her for it. After growing into what I am today and having my own family a simple ADULT explanation would probably clear my packed wound that I call my memories. I get it, I never expected her to be a single mom, working 4 jobs, going to night school, to support putting me through some private school. I just wanted stability or maybe even present minded emotion. My lack of emotional empathy comes from my relationship with my mother. If she ever reads this I hope it helps us both to heal.

As the old saying goes, " I came from nothing so I appreciate everything". A lot of what I went through during my adolescent years shaped and molded me into the driven man that I am today. For that I am thankful, however to this day I cannot bring myself to say the words I love you to her or anyone other then my wife and children (literally ANYONE), I cant sincerely hug her, and I often ignore her phone calls or find an excuse to end them early. Maybe one day all of this will go away and my "mommy" issues will be resolved. Until then I internalize, I write, and I wonder what the truth really is.

FORT LEE, VA

1-3-2016 I am starting the year off in an unexpected manner. I have been in the military now for almost 16 years. My first 11 years were extremely productive and filed with promotions, awards, and tons of training. In the last 5 years I have tried to attend training and work towards getting promoted to the well-established rank of E-8. I am currently serving as the 1SG of the 100th Quarter Master Water Purification Company. That job requires me to hold the MOS of 92F that is a petroleum specialist. I never imagined that I would become a Quarter Master soldier. I have been in the army for 15 years as a Signal Support Systems Specialist. Signaleer's are sincerely a different breed of soldier.

I was given orders on New Year's Eve and told that I would be attending 92F reclassification school at Ft Lee Virginia. The only issue is that my report date was January 3rd. Not very much time at all to prepare the family for my departure, my employer for my extended leave, or myself for the crazy endeavor of jumping back onto an active duty installation. To the untrained individual that may not have ever experienced this before, let me try to help frame this picture for you. The stress of leaving your family is already difficult to adjust to. It always brings about a certain amount of stress and anxiety. I obviously love them dearly and want nothing but the best for them. My civilian employer (the Police Department) is extremely flexible and worked with me. That was a huge plus, as I know that is not the case for many soldiers.

As far as going back onto an active duty installation…. Well that is a very special ordeal. Fort Lee is the home of the Quarter Masters. It is the largest training post for advanced individual training or AIT. There are thousands upon thousands of soldiers that are currently going through the pipeline. Meaning they just graduated basic training and have not yet arrived to their permanent duty station. Most of these soldiers are fresh out of high school and trying to figure out their identity. I have found myself referring to them as kids on numerous occasions. Which is just odd because I'm not very much older than most of them. I have not been on an Army base like this in several years. There are formations marching about all over the place, soldiers shouting cadences, formations and uniforms galore. It is a lot to take in, especially when you have been living your life as a civilian for the last 10 years.

The area that we are training in is cold, there is a special kind of cold that I swear only exist on military installations. The wind cuts through your clothing like a knife into flesh. The air is hard to take in and burns your lungs if you breathe too heavy. It's as if they choose these places on purpose when they decide to build a post. They pick the most baron pieces of land that seem about as miserable, cold, and lonely as you could ever imagine.

1-5-2016

I joined the Army right out of high school, probably the same as most of the kids attending courses here on this base. When I attended technical school we had drill sergeants still assigned to each platoon, we were treated as if we were still in basic training, however we eventually earned our weekends off and minimum liberties within the barracks. Such as the ability to study on our own, more meal options in the dining facility, and if you worked hard enough in class you could earn a weekend pass to exit the post and see the real world on occasion. My time spent going through the US Army Training pipeline was extremely disciplined, rigorous, and tough to get through. Advanced Individual Training (AIT) was 6 months long. Six additional months of not seeing your family or being around anything that you knew as normal. The thing that stands out to me the most on this installation and the newest generation of soldiers is the lack of discipline.

Even though I am here attending a reclassification school they still have us eat chow in the same dining facility as the tech school soldiers. That has been a very strange experience. We are expected to stand at parade rest (a military position that is considered the modified position of attention, your hands are crossed behind your back right over left and your shoulders are held high with your head and eyes affixed straight ahead). When the soldier in front of you moves forward you snap to the position of attention, take one step forward and then go back to parade rest. This may not sound like much, but remember I have been in the military 15 years now. I have served my country honorably by deploying to IRAQ, I am currently the 1SG of a company, and I AM PART TIME NOW. I am basically a civilian that gets to play ARMY from time to time. This action itself has been a weird adjustment. Aside from that we have instructors that are former drill sergeants and expect….no they DEMAND a certain level of discipline that I believe far surpasses that of the pipeline soldiers. I am desperately trying to wrap my head around the entire system and snap back into military mode. It has not been easy at all.

NO FUEL! NO FIGHT! The motto that we must shout before we are allowed to take our seats when attending class. Hooah!!! No alcohol is allowed AT ALL while attending training here at wonderful Fort Lee, Virginia. That means that I will be bone dry until I complete training. That doesn't seem so bad I guess. My body could definitely use the detoxification. I will take this time to focus on training physically and refocusing my mind on the things that matter the most. My Beautiful wife and super amazing kiddos. This actually gives me time to reflect on the things that motivate me and have helped me to achieve the level of success that I have achieved thus far.

REINVENTED ISSUES

5-15-2016 Annual Training with the National Guard is a really big deal. This is typically the largest training event of the year for a unit. My unit is quite unique in the sense that we currently have a dual mission. We are the western regions chemical decontamination team, as well as our normal unit mission of water purification and distribution. Yes, water distribution like the old Pauly Shore movie "In the Army Now". I have been the 1SG of this unit for just under 2 years.

This is my 3rd annual training event with the unit, but my first time essentially running Annual Training. Last year we had a mission in Hawaii as the decontamination unit. The year before that (2014) we drove to Reno, NV and played in the dirt for a few weeks. This training cycle the commander and myself tried to focus more on our regular mission and wanted to give the soldiers an opportunity to use their own equipment. Something that this unit has not done in well over 6 years. We are convoying to Camp Navajo, Arizona. We got approval to use one of their ponds to train water operations. They provided us with a barracks facility and some other Army amenities to call our own for the next few weeks.

This training cycle was supposed to help this unit reinvent itself. We have a lot of young personnel that don't know about the issues from years past. It was going to be an opportunity for the junior leaders to step up and show their ability to lead and take charge. Unfortunately things haven't started out as smoothly as I would have liked. We had 4 AWOL's leading into the day of movement. AWOL is absent without leave.

We approved 5 soldiers to conduct their annual training at another scheduled time; a lot of the requests were pregnancy based. The day of our movement that number jumped to 12 soldiers. Most were valid excuses but there were some lame excuses. It reached a point where myself and the commander were just approving them and letting the soldier flush their own career down the toilet. I figured that if a soldier really didn't want to go with us then I don't want them around. I'm not in the babysitting business and would really prefer to not deal with any additional issues that take away from my ability to properly train those that wish to be trained. It was just extremely frustrating because some of those soldiers are ones that you really hoped would step up and let their potential shine.

JUST A NOTE

6-4-2016 I worked 12 hours of overtime and then loaded the family up for a mini vacation/ beach day. My wife had to drive while I crashed intermittently. It's hard to stay asleep with the constant breaking. Anywho, my son is attending his first college football camp tomorrow. I want him to see what that experience is like early. Maybe that will give him the extra boost he needs to stay focused on his academics. I have realized that athletically he lacks the ability to quit. I think he enjoys the physical rigors associated with competing at a high level. He usually maintains excellent grades as well, but I remember all of the distractions that High-School can toss your way.

DEATH STICKS TO YOU

Growing up in Los Angeles I was no stranger to the site of a dead body. Plus I deployed to Iraq immediately after shock and awe approximately a year and half after graduating high school, so I've seen a dead or mangled body or two. It's not something that I particularly enjoy but unfortunately it has been a part of my existence. Death happens, sadly it happens to the perceived innocent at the most unlikely of times at the hands of willing or unwilling assailants or perhaps there own hands.

My first dead body call on the police department was a vagrant that died behind an alley. He showed signs of rigor mortis and had ants coming from his eyes, nose, and mouth. His pants were soiled as are a lot of people that you find that are deceased. While we were waiting for the coroner to arrive I noticed that he had passed away directly under a No Trespassing sign. I jokingly asked my FTO if I should scratch him out a quick ticket. My FTO looked at me and said "you're a sick fucker... you just might make it through this job".

The coroner's office was taking forever so I popped open the trunk and helped myself to part of my lunch. I learned very early on in training that a hungry cop was a dumb cop. Finally they arrived and did their basic preliminary investigation. Yep, this looks natural. Looks like he drank himself to death. He was surrounded by bottles of Vodka. I asked the dumb question. How do you know that? Don't you see the bottles rookie? Clearly not the answer I was expecting.

This may have been my first dead body call while on the department but it certainly was not my last. I have been on suicides, murders, accidental deaths, natural deaths, fatal auto accidents, and my worst dead baby calls. They all stick to you in one way or another. But babies, those are the ones that I can never seem to shake out of my head. It makes it really difficult to drive through your city. As we pass a place where I've made that long wait for the coroner I instantly remember the death scene.

The dead infant call that still bothers me the most is one that I'll never know the outcome of. I was dispatched to a scene where a mother found her Newborn baby inside of its crib non responsive. When I got there medical was just leaving the scene and they stated that the situation appeared suspicious. I went through my proper

notifications; Supervisor, Coroner's office, Child Protective Services

to see if there were any pending cases involving this family, CSI,

detectives. Before long this tiny apartment was bursting at the seams

with stern uniformed personnel. My job at this point was to watch

over the family.

Once detectives arrived I was there to keep the family calm, answer

simple questions and try to help them cope with their unfortunate

and sudden loss. I was now responsible for watching mom and the

other four siblings in this one bedroom apartment while the

detectives further investigated. While I'm standing in this tiny

cramped living room filled with crying kids and mom I'm trying to

avoid eye contact. It hurts to look grieving family members in the

eyes right after a death. Mom cleaned up this tiny apartment in the

hour that I was there. She must have filled up a solid 4 trash bags.

The detectives were not happy with me for allowing that to happen. I

just figured she needed to keep herself busy.

The baby showed signs of being suffocated. The crib had a ton of stuffed animals and blankets so it was unclear if this was neglect, ignorance, or intentional. That's why this call still bothers me. Was this 5th baby the breaking point and just too much for mom to handle? She managed to get the other four to stay healthy enough to be here today. Was there some other alternative motive or was it sudden infant death syndrome (SIDS). This is the hardest part about patrol work. You rarely get the final answers.

I've seen a few suicides. Mostly shootings and overdoses, I've also personally been on suicide by hanging calls. Those always remind me of scary movies. I've experienced one suicide up close and personal. In a city like Las Vegas we get the occasional jumper from our freeways and large properties such as the stratosphere or inside of the Luxor hotel. People never ask about the self-inflicted gunshot victims or the gun related suicides. They always want to know about the jumpers.

There are three of these incidents that standout for me, as I was the first responding unit on these particular cases. When you arrive first there is always this surge of adrenaline that fills your body and subconsciously you replay the events in your mind over and over again. Thinking about whether or not you could have done anything any differently that would have resulted in the victim living. The first was a white female adult that was in her late thirties. She shot herself in the chest with her boyfriends 45 caliber that he kept neatly tucked behind the bed incase any intruders entered his home while he was sleeping. The boyfriend was mowing the grass in the front yard when he heard that distinctive pop from his handgun. He rushed inside and that's where he found his girlfriend laying in bed taking her final breaths. He immediately dialed 911 and began CPR. By the time I arrived she was deceased. The man's face and arms were covered in blood from giving CPR to a woman that had just shot herself in the chest. The blood was flowing slowly from her mouth and open chest wound.

The firearm was still attached to the bed by a string and just laid there on the side of the bed. The man was in total disbelief. By the time medical arrived she had passed. The Fire Department personnel announced her death at the scene and left her body in place for investigators. A death like this would be considered suspicious circumstances. The entry point of the wound, the location of the firearm, and the presence of the boyfriend all meant that investigators would be called out to the scene. The boyfriend was a bloody mess. After he was photographed he was allowed to clean himself off. A preliminary investigation determined that the lady was suffering from depression and had been heavily medicated. The boyfriend didn't know that she knew where he hid the firearms in the residence. As her family began to arrive it was an emotional scene. As patrol officers our job was to secure the area, protect the crime scene and any witnesses or evidence. We aren't there to console the family or speculate about what happened. It's a terribly awkward position to be in.

As the investigation winds down and the folks in the nice suits begin to leave the amount of uniformed officers on scene also diminishes. Eventually the only folks left are the first responding officer, the owner of the house (the boyfriend) and maybe a volunteer grief counselor who is walking the boyfriend through the next set of steps and trying to help him in anyway possible.

The next suicide as a result of a gunshot wound that stands out would be that of a slightly younger white male adult. He was in his mid twenties and lived with his mother. He too was suffering from depression. However his was brought on by a diagnosed terminal illness. While his mother was in the kitchen putting away groceries after returning from the grocery store he shot himself one time in the stomach.

A single gunshot wound to the stomach can cause all kinds of damage to ones body. This Youngman bleed profusely all over his mother's living room. When myself and other units arrived, he was sitting upright on the couch pale in the face and arms with his mouth wide open. He didn't appear to be breathing, however his eyes were open and they still had a look of life in them. It's a look that's hard to explain or describe to anyone. I assumed he was still alive. We removed the firearm from his hand and secured it, assuming that medical would be taking him to the hospital immediately. When the first responding medical units arrived and saw us standing there they presumed he was dead. I told one of the EMT's on scene "this dude is still alive".

EMT: Naw man that guys dead. Look he ain't breathing.

Me: I'm pretty sure he's alive. Can't you do something or maybe just check to confirm.

Just as I said check to confirm, it was like the man's soul was shouting I'm still in here. He took a breath that was deep and sounded exasperated. It had a slight wheeze to it, almost like an asthmatic. Needless to say it scared the group of first responders, but it got the medical folks all going. They started cutting clothing and loading him onto the gurney post haste. I followed the rig to the hospital, blowing through intersections. I could see them pumping on his chest (CPR I assumed) the entire drive.

Once we arrived at the hospital there was an entire medical team waiting for him. They reminded me of one of those TV drama series about emergency rooms. All kinds of folks were giving directions, calling out numbers, and taping stuff to what seemed like a lifeless body. I peeked at the monitor and saw that he still had a slight pulse. They worked on this young man for about an hour before calling his death.

Now my job is to just sit here with the body in what they call the quiet room. Just waiting for investigators to arrive and do their thing. Sitting in a room with a body that had just passed is eerie yet utterly relaxing in a way. Whatever pain he was suffering was now gone. His lifeless body just lay there on the hospital bed cold from the temperature they leave these rooms at. Not yet stiff but cold. It truly makes you appreciate the time that you have and reminds you that it can all be gone is short moment from one single set of actions. The handgun that he used was a long revolver. It reminded me of a Dirty Harry movie.

The third and final suicide by gunshot that I remember very vividly is a gentlemen that took his own life after his wife left him, he lost his business, and he fell deep off of the wagon all in the same week. The initial call came out as a drunk driver that was hitting parked cars and driving at a slow rate of speed. I was down the road approximately one mile from his current location but in the direction that he was driving. A small white pickup truck driven by a possibly Hispanic male adult that's what I'm looking for.

I setup at the intersection and just wait. It didn't take long but the truck passed me up. I got behind it and initiated my emergency equipment. He paid zero attention to any of that and just kept coasting down the road. Running lights and hitting the occasional parked car. I followed with my lights and siren on and naturally other units were dispatched to assist. Once we had enough units in place we came up with a plan to get the vehicle stopped. One unit would pull in front of the vehicle and simply decrease his speed until the truck stopped. Seemed easy enough!. Once we executed our plan and had the vehicle stopped in the middle of the intersection at Boulder Highway and Desert Inn, a busy intersection, especially during day shift hours.

As I approached the vehicle with every intention of taking the driver into custody he suddenly produced a firearm. Small, revolver, silver, that's all I can remember. I yelled out gun that way all the other officers on the scene knew what I saw. As I yelled gun he placed the revolver to his head and pulled the trigger.

Click... nothing!

He tried again… Click … nothing!

What the hell is going on here was my initial thought. We quickly blocked off the intersection and came up with a tactical plan that would get us closer to him and hopefully get him out of the vehicle before he figured out what he was doing wrong. A small team of officers was assembled and we began to approach the vehicle behind a shield. One officer had a low lethal shotgun, which we planned to use to engage the subject with once we got the door opened. The intent was to use the element of surprise to overwhelm him and then take him into custody. As I approached the door and went to open it the next click was a muffled bang….

His vehicle rolled forward and he lay slumped over the steering wheel. The firearm had fallen to the floorboard. Since I was designated doorman I was still closest to the vehicle. I quickly reached over his body and placed the gearshift into park. We rushed medical forward and got him loaded up and on his way. I later learned that he died at the hospital. He was declared brain dead and his (still wife) instructed the medical personnel to pull the plug.

Inside of the man's vehicle we found a bag of cocaine, a box of shell casing (half suspended and half unused) and a note. The mixed box of shell casings explained a lot. Apparently he had written his final farewell note, snorted a large amount of coke and planned on killing himself in the parking lot of his lost business. He had gotten himself so high that he ended up hitting several cars, which produced the call for service (DUI). When I went to initiate the original car stop after we blocked him in, he loaded the revolver with used rounds and that's why the first few clicks were ineffective. As we were shutting down the intersection, coming up with our tactical plan, and approaching his vehicle the second time, that's when he reloaded the firearm. Some of the rounds were used but unfortunately he picked up one good round and managed to get it loaded.

When he shot himself I knew I wasn't hit. I could see where the firearm was located on the side of his head, on the same side we were approaching from. I just couldn't believe that he had pulled that trigger probably 6 to 8 times and nothing had happened. We figured the firearm was empty or not functional. Murphy's law would have it. As soon as I got there, right next to him, he would figure it out. I was fresh out of field training and finally riding solo when this incident occurred. Despite the trauma, blood, and strange circumstances surrounding the whole ordeal. What I remember the most is what happened after he was rushed away to the hospital. My sergeant at the time walked over to me and said… "You all right"?

Me: Yep, he didn't shoot me sir, so I'm good to go.

Sergeant: Cool, you need to talk to anyone or anything like that?

Me: Talk to anyone? For what? Did I screw up sarge?

Sergeant: Naw man, clear off the event and go handle some calls, they're starting to stack.

Bam! Just like that. I cleared, and went right back to work. I think my next event was a domestic violence call or something run of mill. About 6 or 7 hour later I received a call from a detective letting me know that the guy had died. I asked if they needed anything from me. He said NO! Nothing at all and just like that I instantly felt like I was apart of the twisted law enforcement team. I just assumed that this was how all-tragic events would go. You clear and move onto the next.

The worst murder suicide that still haunts me to this day I'm sure the details of this one will piss you off. The apartment complex where this event occurred is a really busy complex that is filled with tenants. Why it took so long for someone to call the police is still puzzling to me. The husband killed his wife in their bedroom, shot her once in the head. It looked like she was sleeping at the time. Then he walked into the living room, sat on the couch and shot himself in the head. He slumped over and most of the blood was on the floor. A fairly clean scene despite the two pools of blood. Here's the kicker the part that is sure to piss you off. They had a small child in the house at the time of these shootings. A little girl between the ages of 3 and 6. When I opened that door she walked towards me with tears in her eyes, a soggy diaper, and an empty belly. After speaking to neighbors they advised that they heard a few loud pops come from the apartment about two days ago.

This poor innocent little baby had to walk around her dead parents bodies for two days. Wondering why isn't anyone holding me. I'm hungry where's the food? Hey is anyone going to change me? I was furious! This selfish sickened soul could have dropped her off at the front office, wrote the neighbor a note, or phoned a friend. Instead he commits his acts of violence and leaves this cute little face to wonder about for days all alone. We changed her, fed her some McDonald's, and tried to keep her distracted away from the scene at our cars. We all knew. We knew that this baby was scarred for life. We knew she didn't understand it all now, but someday soon she would have to cope with this.

Eventually child protective services arrived and away she went. She took to me for some reason. Maybe it's because I was the first face she saw when we opened the door. Maybe it's because I got the McDonald's and insisted on being the guardian of the nuggets. I'm not sure but I know I'll never forget what her small hands felt like squeezed around my neck as I held her. I'll never forget that final look as I strapped her into that car seat and handed her a plush toy animal from the trunk of my patrol car.

This is one of those calls that you bury deep inside of you and don't tell anyone. How could I explain this to my wife or try to help my kids understand why I hugged them so aggressively when I got home. None of this was easy. Whenever I drive through that particular apartment complex I'm reminded of my nugget buddy and her two dead parents.

CHANCE ENCOUNTER

12-2-2016 Speaking intimately and exclusively about the people that I deal with is unfamiliar for me. However I feel compelled to share this story. Tonight I picked up a last minute overtime gig working traffic control at a busy intersection while the city does construction on the power lines. While working I noticed a black male adult stumbling across the street with his fist balled asking folks for a cigarette. Not too uncommon for this area. He asked a few of the construction employees and eventually one of them obliged.

Afterwards he walked over to a homeless gentlemen hanging around outside of a Del Taco with a dog in a shopping cart. I continued to observe him from a distance just to make sure everything stayed civil. He rubbed the dog's head and exchanged a few words with the homeless guy. A few moments later he stumbled back by and then wandered to the rear of a local bar named Frankie's. Next thing you know I see him driving his car towards a gas station which is parked adjacent to Frankie's. Instantly my thought process was OH NO not a DUI while I'm on overtime. I calmly walked over to his car and asked if I could help him... here is where the story gets really interesting.

He proceeds to tell me while fighting back tears that his friend just killed himself. At first I toss him the standard issued I'm sorry for your loss... then he looks at me and says we served together. The old Army Sergeant in me quickly equated that to...we served in the military together. I asked him what branch and he replied Army. He then explains to me that they joined the military together in Lynnwood California and served together in Afghanistan. I listened... he tells me all about their 2012 deployment as 12B's (combat engineers). I listened... he continues on to explain how they returned home and both moved to Las Vegas as young 20 something's excited to start their life over.... as I listened I noticed... he has chill bumps and his teeth are shattering from the dropped temperature of the Las Vegas winter nights. I ask him if he has a coat and he pops his trunk. There I see a baby stroller. Do you have kids I ask? Yes my son is 8 months old... I listened... he's my life and I would never hurt myself like my friend did....but why? Why would he kill himself like that? I mean were all fucked up from what we saw and did over there.

We talked for a bit and I explained to him that I can see how upset he was and then I ask him if he plans on hurting himself or anyone else. "NOOOO sir, I'm just so...disappointed". I then ask him if I can call anyone for him and he drunkenly removes his phone from his pocket and begins to dial. After about the 5th number he says "I got no one officer". I ask him if I could share something with him and I explain to him my military service, deployment, and the death of my friends... this time he listened. I ask him if he has spoken to anyone and he says no. I then say that maybe it would make him feel better if he took sometime and spoke to someone.

He explains to me that he currently works 2 jobs and that life has been a struggle for the last few years because of all of his mounting responsibilities...I listened but hell, now I can relate. It's almost like I'm looking into a dysfunctional mirror, of broken glass, and if I stare hard enough I can see through the glass shards and into my own hardened soul.

We talk back and forth for a few hours or so. I get him to leave his car parked at the gas station and he walks home which is only a couple of blocks away. I go to shake his hand as he's leaving and he hugs me. This poor broken soul that so desperately needed to communicate his worries to the world. This combat veteran that needed to off load his miserable memories. This American hero that stumbled through traffic at a busy intersection to borrow a cigarette from a construction worker. This guy, on this random night, during this last minute overtime event ended up being the biggest reminder of just how damaged one can be.

Through his suffering and the loss of his friend we met on the 2nd of December. We spoke intelligently about life, we shared our war stories and I truly believe that we both walked away a slightly better person. Appreciative of this chance encounter and understanding of our burden. Best of luck young warrior for greater days are ahead.

PART
II

<u>DICHOTOMY AND DECISION MAKING</u>

Force without wisdom falls of its own weight
- Horace

USE OF FORCE

Reminiscing about the very first time I used force as a police officer, it still feels fresh in my mind. The absolute very first time I used my Batman belt full of tools AND my hands to take someone into custody that clearly had no intention of complying with my commands. Some people would expect a feeling of liberation or power. It was actually quite the opposite. I immediately felt sad for the guy. Please don't misunderstand what I'm saying here. I was 100% justified in my actions and the use of every tool, which I'll get to in a second. I just remember feeling like I wish the guy would have listened or maybe not have been as heavy under the influence as we later learned. I was sad because my use of force on him was totally avoidable by him.

Field training was one hell of an experience. You see I worked in our downtown corridor. An area that was once a hot tourist destination that had become A no man's land due to drugs and heavy gang fighting between the incoming Black gangs from California and the already established Mexican gangs. The area I was patrolling with my field-training officer (FTO) was one of the poorest parts of this ghetto. The details of our call sounded simple enough. A leasing agent was checking on a unit where they had just evicted the resident a few days prior. The evicted tenant had broken back in through a window and decided that he wasn't leaving this time.

When we arrived, with me being in training I took the lead. After a few knocks on the door we could hear the male inside the apartment tossing some stuff around. Technically it's his furniture inside so I figured who cares if he breaks his own property. ROOKIE MISTAKE which came back to haunt me later. We used the key the leasing agent provided us and opened up the door.

Me: SIR Police Department come on out now.

Evicted Tenant: Fuck off I'm not leaving.

... This is where the story picks up a bit and things get interesting. As I scanned the front living room and kitchen area I noticed that the couch had been completely torn apart and its pieces were tossed everywhere. All the dishes in the kitchen were smashed and there was glass and debris everywhere. The apartment had a stench like the bottom of a toilet seat. Clearly I underestimated exactly how much damage this guy was causing to "his own property". The walls had holes from being punched and larger holes from head-butts. The evicted tenant was a white male adult that stood about 5 feet 9 inches tall. He was heavyset weighing roughly 250 lbs and had the build of a bare knuckles boxer of the 1920's. This guy had broad shoulders, an inflated chest, and forearms that clearly have been around a construction site or two. He was balding on the top of his head but his chest lacked no hair at all. With his fist balled he almost resembled an angry, older, much heavier version of Wolverine from the x-men movies.

FTO: You heard him...now what.

Me: Control 3Baker4 Can I get another unit or 2 to my location for an agitated individual.

Evicted Tenant: Get the fuck out of my house. (As he tosses a piece of couch our way)

FTO: You gonna do anything or just stand there.

ME: Hey man chill out and come talk to me. Maybe there's a mistake.

Here's where I realized you cannot reason with drug induced crazy. We exchanged words for several minutes and then he retreated to one of the back bedrooms out of my line of sight. My first thought was… "shit my FTO is not going to like this".

Evicted Tenant: (re-emerges from the shadows with a broom stick and tosses it our way) Get the fuck out nigger pig.

Me: (Did I just hear that right) Hey man that bullshit stops right now. Get over here!

Back up starts to arrive. They come up with a plan to break the back bedroom window and distract him and then ill rush in and grab the guy.

SMASH goes the window. I start to move forward and instead of being distracted, he's laser focused and grabs another piece of couch. Just FYI when a couch is torn apart all the wood has little nails and such hanging from it. I quickly draw my Taser and deploy it. ZAP... ineffective.

Me: Well damn that didn't work

FTO: Try again use your other cartridge.

Me: Dude, drop the couch. ZAP... good contact but this guy is high on something special. He muscles through the second Taser deployment and snatches the probes out of his chest. As I go to tactically retreat my FTO blast the guy in the face with pepper spray. He wipes his eyes with his free hand.

Evicted Tenant: AHHHHH fuck you, blah blah blah (insert more insults).

Now myself and my FTO are standing outside as this pissed off, half tased, pepper sprayed mutant is pacing back and forth between the kitchen and living room. I call the other officer's back up front. Clearly it's time for a new plan. As were discussing our next steps he starts tossing the larger pieces of what's left of the couch out of the window. Now all of the other tenants are starting to come out of their apartments.

FTO: Hey Chuck go to the window and when he sees you the other trainee will hit him with the baton.

Seems reasonable given the circumstances!

Me: (standing at the window far enough away so I can't get hit with a piece of couch) Hey...HEY stop playing man come out the apartment now.

WACK... he takes a solid baton strike to the side of his body and doesn't even flinch. He just kicked back towards the door as if he were swatting an annoying dog away.

Me: yeah that shit didn't work.

About this time the Sergeant who had been monitoring the radio traffic arrives with a low lethal shotgun in hand. He hands it to the other trainee and says if he swings anything else shoot him.

Me: He's coming back!

Evicted Tenant: throws another piece of broken furniture out the window and shouts a few more choice words.

POP... that's the sound a low lethal makes when fired. Almost like squeezing a Pringles container.

All the tenants that are watching freak out. "They shootin him, they shootin him".... one lady screams as she grabs her kid and snatches him back inside their apartment.

The low lethal shotgun definitely had an effect. Not enough but it made him think for a second. He thought about what piece of furniture he was going to throw next. Out came a glass bowl.

POP... now he's pissed.

Sarge calls me over from the window and says, "Were going to go get him, you ready"?

Me: huh... go get him... isn't that what we've been doing.

We stack on the door and he just stands there in the middle of the living room like he knew what was about to happen. Me being the biggest guy and the rookie I get pushed through first. I punch this guy as hard as I can as he's raising his leg to kick me. He slips and we dog pile on top of him. I place him in a department move we were taught in the academy and just squeeze until he falls flat. The Sergeant had already called medical and we called them forward. We rolled him over and I put my handcuffs on him. We load him onto the gurney and he looks like hell. Giant red bruising from the Low lethal on his arm and leg. A huge welt across his stomach from the baton. My first Taser cartridge that was ineffective has one probe stuck inside of his shoulder. The other is dragging behind him. His face still sprinkled with the dye from the pepper spray. This guy got it all and I mean everything. All perfectly articulable based on our policy and procedures at that time. Everything was done within tactical reasoning. As his limp (battered but alive) body rolled away on that gurney my adrenaline started to settle and I was thinking what the hell just happened.

FTO: Yo Chuck go start that paperwork he's gonna need it at the hospital were up for lunch next.

Me: Damn just like that. Yes sir let me wipe this guy's blood off of my shirt real quick.

Just like that back to business. My hands were shaking as I wrote that report. I wasn't nervous or worried in anyway. It was just the adrenaline dump was getting to me. I have been to combat and experienced some crazy fights in my life. But this... this was face to face and purely authority driven. Would I have ever used all of those tools on this guy in a street fight? Absolutely not. In combat would I have to write a report literally minutes after wiping a bad guy's blood off of my shirt? NOPE, not at all! I knew right at that moment that this career was going to be different. Sadly similar in a lot of ways, but different than any other job I have ever done.

A violent professional. That's how I felt in that very moment. Sure it can be written that his actions caused our reactions. His poor decision-making resulted in his hospitalization and ultimately his arrest. Yet in my own head I couldn't help but question if there was another way. In the few months that I served in the downtown area I had a handful of uses of force. None as graphic as this one, but fights, foot pursuits, and uses of force were my introduction to police work.

Our department has evolved in so many ways since that use of force 11 years ago. Could an incident like that occur today? The answer is, YES! However the action would have been slowed down, body cameras would be present, and honestly negotiators probably would have been dispatched and SWAT or someone with far more training then me and my patrol training squad would have initiated contact with the evicted tenant. A much larger emphasis has been placed on de-escalation. Slow the momentum and work through the problem. Use time to your advantage when it is a reasonable option. In this particular circumstance time may have been available. Evaluating the totality of the circumstances is an expectation that is being more critically examined by law enforcement agencies. It's a demand that has been created by public outcry and mass media attention. Is it a good thing? I believe it's a concept that comes with it's pros and cons.

Forcing officers to slow the momentum and think more critically isn't necessarily a bad thing. However judging an officer based upon the decisions made in s split second for the rest of their lives is frightening. No one can say for sure how he or she would respond in a life or death situation until presented with that exact scenario. However quality training and a more well rounded understanding of the situation that you are being presented with can help decrease uses of force. Use of force situation regardless of how minor or major are by far the most stressful situations facing law enforcement officers across the country. We know we have an obligation to protect and to serve. However we also know how far our authority can be stretch. Therefore the responsibility to properly execute that authority lay's heavily on the shoulders of officers. I have never worked with anyone that has said, "Man I hope I get to hurt someone today". That just isn't the case. Officers often have to use force as a reaction to the suspect's actions. Cause and effect! The articulation at the end of these engagements is typically expected to be swift, logical and within reason. The implementation of devices such as Body Worn Cameras will help with this articulation as well as ease the concerns of the citizenry.

PROBLEM SOLVING UNIT

3/15/2012 I started working for a new detail today; it's called the Problem Solving Unit. Our job is to primarily focus on high crime areas within the Southeast Area Command and figure out ways to either eliminate or reduce crime in those areas. It allows us to work in a plainclothes capacity drive unmarked vehicles and develop confidential informants. Plainclothes gives us the ability to walk around neighborhoods and not be easily recognized as law enforcement. It is not the same as being undercover! We always have something identifying ourselves as the police. It just makes people in the community feel more comfortable engaging with us when we are not in uniform. It's one of the best things that I have done since I have been hired onto this police department. The groups of folks that I am working with truly are talented. They each have their own individual strengths and we use that to build off of one another.

One of the guys on my squad is SJ. He is a skinny little Texan that stands at about 5 foot 5 inches. He was an amateur wrestler at one point in his life. In fact, I printed out a picture of him with a belt that he won after a fight and he signed it with "when life gives you shit punch that motherfucker in the face". Besides being one of the best investigators I have ever had, the privilege of working with he is also a hostage negotiator for the department. He is an all American Texan through and through.

Another one of the guys on the squad that I really enjoy working with is Big Man Fry. He stands about 6 feet 2 inches and weighs roughly 280 pounds. He's a massive intimidating man that is not afraid to show you why you should be afraid of him. If you're in a fight or need someone dealt with he's your go to guy. Because of his practiced skills and patience he truly is an asset to the agency. Sometimes we would just sit him in the same room as someone in custody and the fear of his bear paws would calm their demeanor and get them to confess their sins. Which is really strange because he's one of the kindest people I have ever served with. He is mild mannered, compassionate, and a true reflection of what you would expect from a Law Man in your time of need. We responded to a burglary call yesterday and before jumping out of our plain vehicle he had a fully loaded tactical vest with stock piles of ammunition and a shotgun slung to him before I could get the car in park. I often refer to him as Thor.

This squad is filled with personality. One of the guys that I relate to the most is D.T. He rocks an old school throwback VATO mustache. D.T's a smooth talking relaxed soul whose claim to fame is his fatty liver. No joke! Dude can through down some grub and he blames his enlarged liver. It has become a common joke amongst the squad. But not as common as Hanson's mom.

I don't know where it started or why we ran with it for so long. One of the guy's whose last name is Hanson became the butt of all things negative. Whenever anything went wrong we would blame Hanson's mom. On occasion we would walk into our squad briefing room and there would be a cake with a special apology note addressed to Hanson's mom. No one ever claimed responsibility but we all enjoyed the cake. These guys are just a good group of folks that were dedicated to fighting crime. We would often find ourselves hanging out in the area command parking lot for hours after we were released still discussing the madness we had been a part of for the day or talking about the junk we would find during our search warrants.

Some of the warrants that stick out to me the most were warrants served on METH-Head houses. A METH-Head is someone that is addicted to Methamphetamine. Before we executed these warrants we would always make an informal bet on different items we may find. How many torn apart televisions, VCR's, or other gadgets? What's the over/ under on size and amount of sex toys found? Do they shoot (use needles), Freebase (smoke it), or Booty Bump (basically a Meth Enema)? We were always professional while searching and interviewing people, however we found a way to have our fun and try to keep ourselves from going crazy. You would see all kinds of wacked out stuff in drug houses. I distinctly remember searching this skinheads residence once that was suspected of selling Pills and Heroin.

This guy had the most elaborate drawing and sculptures of some truly twisted shit. For example etched glass mirrors that depicted black children being hung or burned. A drawing of voluptuous white women dressed in Viking attire sexually torturing men. Skinheads seemed to always have an abundance of knives, daggers, and throwing axes. But my personal favorite was the literature. I respected their right to possess this culturally cynical filth, but damn some of this stuff was deeply sinister and outright nightmarish. Poems about race mixing and Zionism, books about conspiracy theories taught in schools by the government, pamphlets and flyers that articulated the fact that all niggers were born with AIDS and any sex with them must be dirty sex like apes in a zoo. These dudes were full of shit. I took exceptional pleasure in placing those turds into handcuffs and my new boss would let me conduct their interviews when time permitted. They were always yes sir, no sir when I interviewed them and never brought up their racist views.

My new boss is Frankie, a Cuban guy that is very intense and expects results without any bullshit attached. He has years of experience as an undercover officer in the narcotics section. I have a lot to learn and truly believe that he is the guy that can teach me. He is one of those guys that can get into the head of a criminal and think the way that they think and react to what they are thinking. He always manages to be in the right place at the right time with the right words and attitude to match. He insists that I call him by his first name and "get that sergeant shit out of my head". Ha, what a unique dude operating un-bureaucratically in one of the most bureaucratic businesses in the world. After working with these guys for several years Frankie ended up retiring and opening up a security business somewhere, SJ got hired by the feds and is now one of the agents assigned to help fix that going on in Chicago, and oddly enough Big Man Fry is now a Sergeant and doing great work on graveyard. A bunch of the other folks moved on to work in the Vice/Narcotics bureau or other detective positions across the agency. It was a great squad and one hell of an experience for a young officer.

A CUBAN AND A BLACK GUY WALK INTO A PHARMACY

5/8/2012 Here's a bold statement but it must be said. In 2012 racism is still a thing! Today I experienced one of the more shocking events in my career as a police officer. I've been working in the problem-solving unit now for a few months and have been exposed to the world of surveillance operations. I have been deployed, as a surveillance officer on multiple occasions however tonight was quite different. We were conducting an investigation on a crook in a really prominent part of town known as Summerlin. This guy who Ill call Billy is the son-in-law of a pain management specialist. Billy is a 4 time-convicted Felon who is currently employed by his father-in-law as a marketing director for his medical practice.

So far, into the investigation, we have determined that Billy is stealing prescriptions from the very Doctor's offices that his father-in-law employs him to engage in business relations with. Billy then gets the prescriptions filled at various pharmacies across town utilizing fake ID's. The prescriptions are being billed to legitimate victim's insurance companies and Billy is paying the $5 co-pay and walking away with 180 pills of various painkillers. Most of which have an estimated street value ranging between $20 and $40 a pill. That's right folks that roughly $5500 in pills in one transaction. Here's the kicker, we have evidence that he is doing this at three pharmacies (that's just what we know about).

Tonight we followed Mr. Billy from his residence to a pharmacy where he sat outside in his new Kompressor for 30 minutes until it was too late for the pharmacist to call and verify any of the prescriptions. Mr. Billy then entered the Walgreens and proceeded to place the order. Here's where things get interesting. I entered the store on foot so I could observe Mr. Billy's transaction. While in the store I walked around bought a few things and even informed the manager that I worked for the police department and was conducting surveillance. I showed him my badge and police ID and then continued to conduct my business.

Later on in the evening myself and 2 other Officers entered the store so we could retrieve the video surveillance and talk to the pharmacist. We presented the manager with our police ID and asked him if we could see the video and he agreed. While watching the video, I decided to go outside and update our supervisor. When exiting the store, two uniformed officers greeted me. One of which was from my police academy. They informed me that I had generated multiple calls for service in the area. I read the details and they stated that a black male that was tall, approximately 35 years old, with light colored eyes and braided hair was walking through the store asking questions about the pharmacy and claiming to be an undercover officer.

Let me stop here and explain why I was perplexed with such vexation. The actual crook Mr. Billy has been cashing in fraudulently on prescriptions at this one location since January of this year. That means that he has stolen roughly $20,000 in medication because he has been allowed to refill the prescription every 23 days. I entered the store, identified myself as a Police Officers, and was still seen as a bigger threat to the store. Dressed in a Hawaiian print t-shirt with some jeans, my hair was indeed not braided and I properly identified myself, and most importantly I was there to help you. In fact, they took my picture and documented the time that I entered and exited the store. One of my partners noticed the printed pictures of me on the manager's desk and asked if we could have them. When we showed him the actual bad guy he was totally shocked and acted as if there was no way it could be true. You see Mr. Billy is a white male that was wearing a purple shirt and tie so there is no way he could be a threat. As irritated as I was by the manager's blatant racism, I maintained my professionalism.

My boss Frankie's attitude about the whole thing was basically screw that guy and his preconceived notions. If it weren't for the Cuban and black guy his poorly run pharmacy would have been robbed blind. I still laugh about this one from time to time when I link up with the guys from that squad. As sad as it may be, it's our reality. In the end we issued warrants for Billy's arrest and took him into custody outside of a different pharmacy nonetheless. While searching his vehicle we found a police scanner, a briefcase full of prescriptions, several magazines in Russian and aircraft magazines. Apparently this guy was a spy in his own mind. He spoke limited Russian (self-taught) and was taking flying lessons. We believe he planned on transporting his pills to other states, maybe even countries. This one felt right!

CONCRETE PREACHING

10/12/2013 Doing a little concrete preaching today... Some 16-year-old kid that wants to drop out of school was hanging out in front of a liquor store bright and early on a Saturday morning, smoking cigarettes. We talked about what his future would more than likely consist of if he continued down his current path. One of my partners arrived and said the following statement that really sums up my interaction with most people throughout the day...he stated that" the front bumper of a patrol car can be a lot like the pews of an abandoned church".

Whispers of past experiences, advice given to broken souls, and heavy counseling sessions have all occurred in the front of my patrol car. A lot of what we do in law enforcement is centered on the concept of helping people. Some officers are better than others at this part of the job. Street preaching is what some of us call it. Man why would you waste your time preaching to that guy/gal they don't care about what you're saying! With most folks this may have been the case, but the small chance of reaching one person or changing the perception of the police, is worth all the concrete and street preaching.

Listening to someone's story can be one of the best things you can do for some people. Often times they just want to get the information out and let someone know who they are and that they exist. We meet people every day in our profession and don't usually have the time to spend to listen to everyone's life story. When it's relevant we find ourselves trying to get the person to hurry up and spit out the stuff we need while skipping over the added extras.

I met a homeless guy once that swore he was a graduate of MIT. That's right the Massachusetts Institute of technology. Here's his story. Dylan was hanging out behind a 7/11 near some dumpsters that are labeled with signs that read No trespassing NRS 207.200. I was bored so I figured why not stop by and strike up a conversation. Dylan immediately stood out from the crowd because he was articulate and well spoken, very respectful, standoffish but respectful.

Me: where are you from Dylan.

Dylan: MIT sir.

I thought to myself okay ill play his game.

Me: What's MIT Mr. Dylan does that stand for something.

Dylan: you know the school. For smart math people.

Me: huh, oh yeah what's 56 multiplied by 137.

Dylan: 7672 (without a breath or the wink of an eye)
The other homeless dudes hanging out enjoying the show start to chuckle!

Me: That's a cool trick. How'd you do that?

Dylan: I have this thing with numbers. That's why I went to MIT.

Me: Ok-ok, now I'm interested what's your deal my man. Why is that brain sitting behind a 7/11 in Las Vegas wasting away?

Dylan then explains to me that his parents were from the Boston area and had money. Old money as he called it! Dylan got accepted to MIT and was doing well in his studies but he wanted to "live up" the college experience. He got involved in drugs. A little weed at first, then pills; eventually he tried the hard stuff but hated it and settled in on weed. One day he was hanging in his small apartment and some "friends" stopped by and asked if Dylan could get them a large amount of weed for a party they were headed to. Dylan didn't want to disappoint so he called his guy, who ordered him a bag of some premium product. Next thing you know Dylan is being placed under arrest and taken to jail. He says his parents bailed him out, hired an attorney to fight the whole thing and "make it go away" but then they cut off his trust fund and told him they wouldn't support him and his drug habit. Dylan proceeds to tell me that he went to the bank took out his last bit of money. Purchased a ticket to Las Vegas because he figured he would make cash here with the gambling and all. Well clearly that didn't work out and now he's homeless wondering the streets just trying to figure some stuff out.

Dylan: what's today's date sir.

Me: why you got a hot date or something.

Dylan: no sir my mom's birthday is the day before Halloween.

Me: well it's getting close to that.

I took a chance because I thought the story was pretty clever, even if it weren't true. I offered to let Dylan call his mom from my cell phone. He damn near cried. Of course Mr. "I have a thing with numbers", had her number memorized. He dialed and there was no answer. As he went to hand me the phone back, I told him to try again and leave a message. He walks around for a bit and then decided to give it a shot. Again no answer! So he leaves a message.

Dylan: Thank you sir, that meant a lot to me. I just really wanted to wish my mom a happy birthday.

Me: No problem numbers, seeya around, and stay away from weed, that shit ruined your life.

Dylan: haven't touched a joint since.

We part ways and I drive off to my next call for service. Several hours later my phone rings and its Dylan's mom. She received the voicemail and called the number back. I explained to her who I was and how I met her son. She was shocked to hear that he was in Las Vegas. After they cut off his trust fund he just disappeared. It had been several months since she heard from him. Curiosity got the best of me so I had to ask. Ma'am, did Dylan really go to MIT. She laughs and says, YES! He was always different and seemed to never forget numbers. She said he wanted to be an engineer or something like that, but got in trouble and that her and her husband refused to support him if he was engaged in those types of activities.

I drove back to the 7/11 where I had previously stopped Mr. Numbers and no one was there. I asked the clerk is he knew where the group of homeless folks disappeared to and he replied the hell away from here. Not helpful at all. I drove around and looked for Dylan with no luck. People in his position would often drift around town before either being arrested for some small violation or eventually leaving Vegas. I learned something very valuable from this minor street preaching expedition. Always treat people like people, because you never know who you may be dealing with. Dylan could have been a paranoid schizophrenic or he could have been a former Senators son. None of that mattered to me. I took the conversation at face value and just treated him with the same amount of respect that I would treat anyone until they give me a reason otherwise. I never ran into Dylan again.

WORST ACCIDENT EVER

5/15/2012 52, that's the number of fatal accidents that have occurred here in Las Vegas. Unfortunately, I was the first to find the body of number 52. Ill start by attaching the preliminary news article that was published by the Las Vegas Review Journal.

One killed, one arrested in fatal hit-and-run accident

LAS VEGAS REVIEW-JOURNAL
Posted: May 16, 2012 | 6:22 a.m.
A man was killed and another man was arrested Tuesday night after a fatal hit-and-run pedestrian accident in the southeast valley.

Police said a man crossing Nellis Boulevard near Flamingo Road about 11 p.m. Tuesday was struck by a 1997 Nissan Altima. The man was not in a crosswalk and died at the scene.

The driver of the Nissan, left the scene but was later located and arrested by police officers on suspicion of drunken driving.

This was the 52nd fatal traffic accident in Las Vegas jurisdiction this year.

The details of the incident as I remember it are actually quite brutal. At around 2300 hours, I was conducting surveillance in the area of Boulder Highway and Nellis. I was parked on the southeast side of the property. My partner and I were watching an apartment where a suspected robbery suspect was staying. We heard a very loud thump that caught both of our attention. We looked around and saw nothing suspicious. There were no stopped cars in the road, no damage to any walls or buildings. We both just figured that maybe someone tossed an extremely large item into one of the dumpsters that was located directly behind us.

Curiosity got the best of me and I insisted that we drive around to further investigate. We drove through the property once and saw nothing. On our second loop around the property, I looked to my east and saw what appeared to be a person lying near a fire hydrant. What struck me as odd was the fact that this person didn't appear to be moving, and was lying in an awkward position. I exited our vehicle and started to approach the person, that's when I realized that it was a lifeless body wrapped around the fire hydrant.

I walked back to my car and my partner just handed me my handheld radio. My radio traffic sounded something like this.

Me: Control 8K6 can you copy a 401A.

Control: Go ahead

Me: There's a man down on the eastside of the property. Can you roll medical and a few patrol units?

Control: Copy

Exiting my vehicle again and approaching the body for further examining, I quickly realized that he was already deceased and there was nothing that could be done. Ill do the best I can to paint a picture of this horrific scene. His back was facing the hydrant, what was left of his head was turned in slightly towards the brick wall that was built to protect the hydrant from vehicles. His legs and feet were facing upward when they should have been facing towards the east. He was essentially twisted at the mid-section. His hands were folded under his body. There was an extremely large pool of blood all along the rear portion of the wall. A closer look revealed that the back of his head was missing, in fact it was hollowed. A hollowed head usually means no brain. My partner and I looked around and discovered the missing contents of the victim's head. There was brain matter spread out roughly 50 to 75 feet from the body over an area of about 50 yards. It looked as if the inside of his head was exposed to a blender with no top, and all of the contents had flown all over a kitchen.

We immediately started shutting the area down to preserve the crime scene. While placing police tape around the area, my partner found a piece of the victim's brain that was about the size of a standard size apple or orange. Chaos is really the only word that can begin to describe any accident scene, but this one was particularly brutal. It reminded me of some of the destructive scenes I was around during my time in Iraq. It had the resemblance of an IED explosion or a headshot from a large caliber firearm.

It is usually difficult to sleep after seeing such terrible things. Each of us have our own way of dealing with such tragedy and destruction, some use humor, others have their own personal vices. I like to believe that I have my own Pandora's Box of bad crap tucked deep away in the back of my head. I'm sure that at some point that box will begin to overflow and all of the world's nastiness that I have been exposed to will consume me. Maybe that will be the day that I resort to vices instead of more practical measures. I love the work that I do, but I am also realistic and I realize how damaging it can.

CULTURAL CHALLENGES

7-7-2016 It has become extremely difficult to watch the hatred towards law enforcement. At times I question whether or not I too am a part of the systematic destruction of impoverished neighborhoods, despite the fact that I DO NOT police with arrogance or hatred in my heart. I try to be as fair and impartial as possible. I choose to personally approach each situation independently and simply **treat people like people**. I would love to say that each officer that also bears the burden of the badge polices objectively.

Unfortunately that is not the case. I am frustrated beyond belief and feel torn for so many reasons. I am a police officer, a minority police officer, a Black police officer. Very few people that know me know of my profession. I share this with few people for several reasons. I do not want to be judged based upon the actions of others across the country that share the same profession as me. Questionable shootings and uses of force have become everyday stories for major media outlets, social media streams, and gossip columns. The days of waiting for fact-finding reviews, court appearances, and witness interviews are over. Our country has now become a nation that instantly passes judgment based upon video footage that is immediately released and cameras that are tossed into the faces of the emotionally distraught. It is the harsh reality of our current operating environment.

In my chosen professions both in law enforcement and the military I have always focused on problem solving. We can identify problems all day long, but at some point we have to be willing to figure out how to come up with solutions to those problems. Apart of problem solving is the dissection of the issue at hand. Problematic police encounters exist because there is a bridge that must be gapped between the police and the communities they are responsible for protecting. Here are some of the ways that I can see agencies across the United States bridging that gap.

- Updated and improved hiring standards: employment history should not be as large a factor, minor credit violations should not be a factor, and prying into personal relationships over the use of low level narcotics shouldn't be standard practice. If the federal government has taken a stance to ignore marijuana as a level 2 narcotic why do police agencies permanently disqualify minority recruits for their past usage of marijuana?

- Hire more Veterans: most veterans that serve within the armed forces have had the luxury of serving in a culturally diverse work force. They are typically better at communicating clear and concise commands, following orders from the chain of command (no rogue policing) and they understand the sensitive nature required to handle certain scenarios

- Hire more LOCAL employees that represent the community being serviced. If we hire people that attend the same church groups, grocery stores, schools, and social events then we are hiring not just an employee but also a trusted source within the community. By hiring Locals that reflect the community they will serve we are saying that we truly UNDERSTAND and ACKNOWLEDGE the fact that some communities are certainly different than others. Not that we must enforce certain laws in some communities but not others. Simply that the manner in which we enforce those laws would vary.

- Stronger emphasis on community based policing. The more opportunities an officer has to interact with the citizens within a community outside of negative police encounters the better the potential outcome will be during those negative or harsh encounters.

- Lastly we must stop placing all POLICE agencies into a bubble. The vast majority of issues that are occurring are taking place in communities with smaller law enforcement agencies that may not have the same quality of training, the same working relationships, or the same characteristics as some of their neighboring agencies to include larger metropolitan agencies. Larger metropolitan police agencies recognize these issues and have the manpower, budget, and volunteerism in place to facility change.

No one is expecting perfection, however everyone expects accountability. Accountability is something that I can openly admit is largely lacking within the law enforcement community. After all, it takes time to retrain a guy, and it takes time to properly document all of his misfortunes and misguided arrest, it also takes time and lots of effort to supervise the supervisors and ensure they are properly documenting these incidents. Law enforcement agencies across the country have become more administrative in nature based on the demands of the local and federal governments. I absolutely understand that there is a need for this. However it appears that we have failed to properly promote true leaders within law enforcement agencies that are willing to have those tough conversations with their troops.

We lack leaders with voices that are willing to standup to the current operating procedures and say this IS NOT WORKING. We have mid-level supervisors that are excellent pushers of broken policies that do not effectively help us police ourselves yet alone the streets. Leadership is a whispered word amongst the halls of many law enforcement agencies because how do you measure someone's leadership. What quantifiable actions must one take to be considered a leader in Law? The simple memorization of a policy manual does not constitute an effective leader, nor does it help a broken or damaged police officer learn, grow, and improve within this profession. Everyone has become so focused on political correctness that we have forgotten human effectiveness. If agencies fix their leadership problems, that will have a direct impact on the communication problems that exist.

The blue line is a myth. It doesn't exist anymore. It has been replaced by a clear-coated sound barrier, which lack the ability to reflect. We cannot speak out publicly without the fear of being shamed by our fellow comrades or potentially punished by our agencies. Instead we are silenced and pretend that doubt does not exist. It may not be affecting me directly, but in a very indirect manner it certainly affects us all. For those of us that work in law enforcement and share the same characteristics as the many victims of the high profile shootings (Black or Hispanic, young, or urban) we find ourselves torn. Torn between our chosen professions and our cultural identities.

Being myself at work doesn't seem to be an option. Despite my DEGREE's (yes that's plural) if I show my cultural strength whether that be through my clothing, haircuts, or choice of music I am instantly snared upon. It may not always be verbal, but the stares and request to verify my employee identification speak volumes louder than any words ever spoken. So I/we sit back, we execute our given task, and simply pretend that we are not a part of the obstacle, because after all I haven't killed any innocent, unarmed people!

What keeps me focused and helps me maintain my faith in humanity are my kids and their innocence. My son and I will often engage in deep conversations about civility and common occurrences. I am constantly reminded that things just aren't that bad. Like me explaining to my son why he should be careful when engaging with law enforcement officers that don't share his pigment and him explaining that he doesn't have to worry about that because he doesn't plan on interacting with the police at all. My kid's remind me that the world isn't always a place filed with judgment and preconceived notions. The bonds they share with their woven mixed race of friends with varying personalities introduces the most vibrant dichotomy into a police officers life that one could ever conceptualize.

JUST A NOTE

8-22-2016 Been grinding and working all kinds of crazy hours over the last few weeks. I have taken pretty much every overtime gig that

I can find. Consuming myself with work isn't new to me, I am no stranger to hard work, however in doing so I have missed out on a few things happening at home.

Sitting around during lunch after taking care of my morning tasks. I decided to catch up on some social media shenanigans. As I was scoping out Snap Chat I see that my son has dyed his damn hair… Have I really been that disconnected from my own family that I didn't know that my own son has dyed hair? Have I become an absent father within my own home? Have I really become the provider that doesn't exist? The dad that's dad via water, power, and mortgage minus the guidance and present living conditions. This really sucks!!! No other way to put it.

This is terrible, but let it be acknowledged, accepted and never forgotten. I refuse to not be there for my children and my wife. I have fought so hard to have the things that I never knew existed when I was child. I want to provide and give them the world, but I also want to experience it with them. I know it's possible to do both. I know I can manage it all. I have to focus, prioritize my time, and stay as connected as possible. Presence is by far the best form of parenting I can ever provide. It's the largest piece of the puzzle that was missing from my childhood and I can see myself starting to follow that trend. Definitely not as extreme as my childhood, but nevertheless not being there is not an acceptable parenting practice.

PART
III

ENFORCEMENT AND CORRECTIONS

"The privilege of the writ of habeas corpus shall not be suspended, unless when in cases of rebellion or invasion the public safety may require it."
Article I, Section IX of the U.S. Constitution

YOUR OWN DAUGHTERS

11-16-2010 Some calls stick to your brain like a loose sneeze on a window and just want go away. This one angers me beyond belief. We received a welfare check call for service from Child Protective Services. The details of the call explained that they had received a call from a women's correctional facility in Arizona. A mother that was incarcerated for attempting to smuggle narcotics across the border wanted officers to check on her two daughters. The daughters are currently living with their father while mom goes through the deportation process.

The two girls were 11 and 8 years old. The 11 year old was extremely mature in personality and clearly had taken on the mother role in this home. The 8 year old was quiet, scared, and standoffish. Both girls displayed a certain since of independence that upon arrival let you know that something wasn't right in this apartment. Mom called from prison to checkup on the family one evening and her 11 year old daughter whispered to her "he's doing it again". Mom immediately knew exactly what was happening while she was away.

Dad had a special way of showing his love and affection for his daughters. When his 11-year-old daughter was younger, possibly around the age of 6 or 7 her father had been sexually molesting her. The mother caught him in the act one day having sexual intercourse with his daughter. She said that he begged her not to call the police because they would be deported and he would go to jail and split up their family. He promised her that he would never do it again. Somehow mom believed him and never reported the incident. Fast-forward several years and now that mom is incarcerated and temporarily out of the picture dad decided that he wasn't going to be alone at night for long. He began having sex with his oldest daughter again. The sex acts that this filthy individual had his own daughter performing on him were foul and quite frankly flat out disgusting. The 11 year old figured that as long as his efforts were focused on her then he would leave the 8 year old alone.

Well one day the 8 year old wasn't feeling well so dad kept her from school. When his oldest daughter returned home from school she noticed that her sister was crying and clearly upset. She was so upset that she refused to speak and just cried herself to sleep. The 11 year old was doing laundry later on that evening and came across a bloody pair of her sister's underwear and immediately knew what occurred. Apparently dad got lonely while the 11 year old was at school and decided that his youngest daughter would be a suitable substitute. After several hours of dealing with this poor child she finally broke down and described to the detectives what sounded like hours of multiple sexual encounters by her father.

When the 11-year-old answered moms call she knew that was her only chance to say something and hopefully get help. She was absolutely terrified to tell anyone at school from fear of judgment by the other kids if anyone overheard her. The thought of these poor children living through this nightmare still pisses me off to this day. How can a man even find himself to be sexually attracted to children? Even worse how can a father molest his own daughters?

I can still remember with clear distinction the look on that poor child's face when she opened the door. She appeared relieved yet frightened. Somehow she kept it together and stayed strong looking after her little sister during the entire process. I was assigned the duty of watching over the dad who spoke very little English. Judging by the look on his face he understood why we were there yet he remained calm and acted as if the whole thing was no big deal.

The Spanish interpreter that we had present with us was visibly upset. She was fighting back tears as I asked her to translate to the father that we would be taking his daughters and doing an investigation. I told him that he would be getting detained based on the initial statements made by mom and the daughters. He agreed in an almost smug manner and just turned around and pointed his hands in my direction. The interpreter translated… Take me if you want, but they're my daughters. I bit my tongue and tried my hardest to remain professional as to not jeopardize the case. I thought to myself YOUR DAUGHTERS. How can this savage honestly feel that he deserves the right to call these two tortured little faces his daughters? The girls packed up a few things and gladly exited the residence with CPS workers.

The thing that hurts the worst about these types of calls is that you rarely get to know the end result. We do our small part, take the initial reports, and clear the call with comments. Maybe it's better that I don't know where dad is or what happened to him. Perhaps it's better that we aren't involved long enough to grow any attachment to the victims.

Either way the call still sticks with you and you can't just un-hear the words of disgust spoken by the kids. You can't justify the smug ignorance that the father expressed and you can't help but wonder whatever happen to the mother and if she ever got reunited with her daughters. Often times an Officer will clear a call like this and then move onto the next call for service. I can't remember what I did after this call. I know that it wasn't as important and can never have the same impact on me as the faces of those two little girls. Unfortunately this is the way the world works for a police officer. You call, we respond, hopefully we help, sometimes we don't, but either way we move onto the next event.

THE DITCHING MATH MAJORS

12-8-2010 During the holidays the department takes a huge stance against robberies and other person crimes, specifically in the shopping areas all across town to include the malls and Walmart's. During this time all of the squads are mandated to provide a certain amount of officers to be H.I. units. H.I. meaning holiday initiative

Today I was assigned as 2HI21, my area of responsibility was the Walmart located on the Boulder Hwy and Flamingo. A pretty popular shopping destination, which is also infamous for its purse snatches, petit larcenies and cart runs. So needless to say my presence in the old faithful black and white patrol car definitely served its purpose. After all, officer presence is the first line of defense in the use of force continuum. My sole purpose in life was to drive around this particular area for my entire 10-hour shift.

At around 1100hrs or so I started to feel like I was on my last lap so I decided to break up the monotony and patrol around the park, which is located directly across the street and conveniently tucked away behind a church. As I approached the church I could see 3 people sitting on the benches. It was obvious they had noticed me as well because upon my arrival they got up and started to walk away.

The closer I got to them the easier it was to make out their ages. All of them looked to be about 17 years old or younger. Two Hispanic female juveniles and one Hispanic male juvenile. Being as how it was only 1100hrs I knew they should have been in school. I immediately executed a U-turn and engaged my lights while calling the stop out.

Me: Control this is 2HI21 copy a 468 3 times at Maslow Park.

Control: 2HI21 copy

Me: Control 2HI21 I'm code 4

All three walked over to the front of my car before I could even get out and tell them to. "How old are you," I asked.

I pointed to the kid on the farthest left.

Kid 1: ummmm I'm 18 mister

"REALLY" I thought to myself, as my bullshit meter started to boil over. I repeated the question to each one them and got the same response all three times. Okay ill play your silly little game. "What school should you be at right now?"

Kid 1: who us ummmmm I mean we didn't graduate. We just dropped out.

Um huh, so let me get this straight all 3 of you look like you're 15 but you all are 18 and have already dropped out of school….interesting. Ok "ill entertain you for a while". I say. "What's your birthday"?

Kid 1: 12-3-89

Kid 2: 10-16-89 "He shouted this out quickly as if rehearsed".

Kid 3: looked around a bit then replied with 1-5-89

At this point I knew they were definitely lying. You see its 2010 which means that if they were born in 1989 they would all be 21 and not 18. Because I'm a nice guy so I offered them an opportunity to correct their math.

Me: Are you sure that's your birthday.

Kids: Simultaneously yes mister that's it... as they look everywhere but in my direction.

Ok kids here's the deal, I'm not fond of playing games so you have two options. Option one is you can all tell me your real names and birthdays and ill call the school and verify that you actually go there then I'm dropping you off. Or option two, you can continue to lie, Ill call the school police, they will put you in handcuffs, take you to jail and probably write your parents truancy citation. So before I get upset I'm going to ask for the final time how old are you.

Kid 1: 15 mister.

Kid 2: looks at the ground I'm 17 but I really do go to adult ED because I dropped out for ditching last year. I only had 9th grade credits.

Kid 3: I'm 16 but please don't arrest me mister I just wanted to eat some pizza for lunch and not that stuff they serve at school.

Me: I appreciate your honestly, now standby while I call the school to verify. Its not that I don't trust you, it's just that…well I don't really trust anyone.

After a brief conversation with the school police officers they verified that all of the information that I was finally given was correct. I let the adult ED kid go home and drove the other two to school and wished them luck in their math classes because it was obvious that they needed it.

NEW YEAR'S ON THE STRIP

1/1/11 HAPPY NEW YEAR! BOOM POW FLASH as the fireworks exploded overhead and all of the digital cameras and cell phone capture the magic that is Las Vegas on New Year's. I can't help but to thank about my family that is sitting at home welcoming another new year without me being present. I continue to scan the crowds for anything that may be suspicious. After all I have been inundated with information over the last few weeks from several intelligence agencies that recommend a heightened level of vigilance in America particularly in larger metropolitan areas such as Las Vegas. This is prime real estate for psycho fascist, anti-American, anti-democratic, and anti-freedom terrorist.

My entire squad stood in our pre assigned positions in front of the imperial palace and scanned our sectors. Some people took pictures of us, some threw bottles, but very few thanked us. Those that did typically stated that they appreciated us keeping them safe on New Year's. Most followed that statement up with "I don't see how you guys do it, this is crazy". Crazy indeed my friends. The police are outnumbered probably 10,000 to 1 on the strip and that's no exaggeration. The fact that all serious incidents have been completely eradicated prior to any citizen even realizing that it exist can only be attributed to the fact that this agency truly is one of the best in the world.

Every suspicious activity call is immediately investigated, suspicious packages are handled with care, and drunks are tamed and sent on their way ALL NIGHT LONG. This is the most tolerable night of the year for our agency. We break up fights and the thought of a citation or arrest rarely cross your mind because of how chaotic the atmosphere is around you. So instead we usually separate the parties involved and have them walk one north and other south on opposite sides of Las Vegas Boulevard. Unless it's domestic related of course. Don't let me fool you, we do make arrest on this night but it takes a lot to talk yourself into handcuffs on New Year's in Las Vegas.

Let me set up the scene for you. First of all no one and I do mean no one is off within our organization on this night. All of the light duty officers are assigned less stringent post such as guarding area commands or watching access tunnels. Every area within the valley still has sufficient coverage to handle calls for service because believe it or not, not everyone goes to the strip to bring in the New Year. At approximately 1530 hours most squads meet and load up all of their gear into pre assigned patrol vehicles. Then we have one final meeting to ensure accountability and to get briefed on any last minute changes or added threats.

After everyone is loaded into their transportation whether that's a county bus, a patrol vehicle, or one of our unmarked secret squirrel cars, we drive down to our designated assignment on the strip. Upon your arrival you are again briefed only this time it's by whatever lieutenant is in charge of your area of operation. The lieutenant will let you know where the bathrooms are located, the arrest stations, the warming station (if you're lucky enough to have one) and the casino employee dining facility where you can grab a quick bite to eat. This is a necessary part of the evening especially due to the fact that not everyone works on or anywhere near the strip. We will then split into teams and no one is allowed to leave the area without their partner. This is the best way to ensure that none of us get over taken by the crowds and separated from the group. Each squad of officers will then be released to their Sergeant and will eat when told to do so.

This is where things begin to get exciting. At around 1800 hours or so we completely shut down the strip. No vehicles other than ours are allowed access to Las Vegas Boulevard. We start at the far south end of the strip and take over one intersection at a time. Patrol vehicles with lights and sirens stop all flow of vehicle and pedestrian traffic and then we move barricades into the street allowing pedestrians to walk on both the sidewalk and usually one or two lanes of traffic. The streets fill up quickly and madness ensues. The entire street of Las Vegas Boulevard is shut down in a matter of minutes and the streets are covered with people, beer bottles, trash, and who knows what else instantly. All of the street performers pop up out of nowhere and begin to sing, dance, and act for money. Their buckets and hats fill fast. People selling beads and flashing lights from trash bags are spotted at every angle. It's almost as if there is 1 person selling something for every 5 people that are just there for a good time. Most of the casinos have live DJ's performing in front of them and the night clubs begin to sell alcohol by the case load right on the corners.

It's amazing how fast it all unfolds. If we shut down the streets at 1800hours by 1830 it's a full-blown rave. There's music blasting from every angle THUMP THUMP THUMP ranging from hip-hop, rock, and techno to acoustics and Frank Sinatra. There are religious protestors with signs that read THE LORD IS YOUR SAVIOR don't sin in this city that are holding giant 5x10 foot signs with bull horns shouting various scriptures from different religious books. All of the people in costume appear out of nowhere and Las Vegas truly does become an adults Disney Land.

3-2-1 Happy New Year. 10 minutes after the fireworks erupt the crowds begin to fade as we push the barriers back towards the sidewalk and take our cities beloved strip back under control. If only we could leave as fast as we came. The night for us will not end for many more hours. We stick around and guard the street vending clubs and businesses until about 0200 hours. Then the great lights of the south as I like to call them can be seen. Approximately 20 traffic motorcycles, 10 street sweepers, 15 trash trucks, and about 100 public works employees line the street and begin the long walk north. The entire strip is driven from south to north and every bit of trash is picked up and the street swept. It takes about an hour and Las Vegas Boulevard is back to normal. We all load up into our chariots and escape back to our respective head quarters to be debriefed and released. 0430 hours this year, not bad at all. By 0600 hours I was at home and ready for bed. I had enough of Adult Disney Land and was ready to crash out.

CANADIAN AND SUCH

1/15/11 Last night I worked at ROK Vegas, which is located inside of the NY/NY Casino on the fabulous Las Vegas Strip. Typically when I work at places like this its over-time and the only thing they expect of you is your officers' presence. They basically pay a fee to the department in order to have two uniformed officers on property in the event anything occurs that requires police action. These are usually easy over-time gigs and require very little work. On rare occasions you do get the occasional drug arrest, domestic violence or other disturbance calls, but mostly drunk and disorderly calls.

The night was going well. I was working with my over-time partner Officer P. The most interesting thing that occurred all night was him meeting several groups of people all of which were from Minnesota but none of them were there together. I'm attributing the fact that Minnesota is basically buried under a mountain of snow for this massive influx of Minnesotians.

Before I go any further let me explain Officer P to you. He is an extremely charismatic black male who stands about 5'10 and weighs approximately 180 pounds. He's in his mid 30's and recently separated from his long time girlfriend of 10 years. They have 2 handsome boys together and split on fairly even terms. P being the newly single guy that he is has found that he particularly enjoys stretching his single guy legs and running a flirtatious marathon at a full sprint. Every woman that walked by he threw them a smile and most of them make it a point to stop and walk back to let him know that he looked very attractive in his uniform. By the end of the night he must have gotten more compliments then a prize-winning stallion.

In fact I'm sure he would consider himself a stallion of some sort. Don't let me confuse you though. He's still an absolute professional, after all or job is to serve and then protect as he says. So whenever someone asks if we can take pictures with them he dives at the opportunity while I try to avoid cameras at all cost. I prefer to be left alone while in uniform. There's just a part of me that enjoys people thinking that we are hardened, mysterious, protectors of the city. It's a façade that I like to think that I manage well. All I can say is that my partner enjoys the attention but he handles is well. Watching him work a crowd of people over is amazing. I often joke with him by calling him the new face of our department.

Our shift was scheduled from 2230 until 0430 hours. The nightclub shut down at 0330 hours, which meant that we were able to go down to the employee-dining restaurant (EDR) and grab a quick bite to eat while sitting down and resting our feet. Most of the casinos are designed like mazes beneath the lower levels. After being escorted through the tunnels like rats chasing the scent of cheese we finally arrived at salvation. My feet were aching bad tonight for some strange reason and sitting down was going to be a great feeling. We buzzed ourselves in with the badge they had given us earlier in the night and preceded to fix a plate of food. I made a salad and grab a piece of prime rib. Not bad eating considering the price of free. P chose the chicken fingers route and grabbed a salad as well. We headed towards a seat at the end of the EDR and that's when it happened. The security director walked in and told us we had a situation to handle on the upper level.

Naturally my first thought was really, all night nothing happens and the moment I go to sit down BAM. We passed our plates along to some of the employees that were on break. As we headed upstairs he began to explain the "situation" to us with great exuberance.

> We have a lady upstairs at the American Café that's refusing to pay her bill. Yeah, my guys are up there now with her in custody. You know these people
>
> Come here from all over the place and think they can get away with whatever they want while in Vegas. Well not this time, we caught her HA.

The security director was truly excited by this misdemeanor offence of defrauding an innkeeper, without ever getting the details of what exactly occurred. He went on and on and on as we took the long walk back through the maze, up the stairs, and through the casino floor. Typically if we were not present they would have handled this situation any number of ways, depending upon the circumstances.

Officer P and I walked up to the four, that's right I said four casino security personnel that were standing in front of the "suspect". Officer P got their side of the story meanwhile I talked to the offender. She was a white female who had some obvious physical deformities as half of her face appeared to not be functioning. Her skin was flaky and peeling. She was red from what appeared to be too much sun exposure despite the fact that it was only 50 degrees on the strip that day. I began talking to her and her breath reeked of alcohol. Her speech was slurred and she had a bit of an accent. After a brief conversation it was discovered that she was a Canadian who was traveling with a shuttle of other vacationing Canadians. The only form of money she had on her person was a pre-paid debit card. The only form of ID she had was her passport. She had no friends or family that she traveled with. She was terrified and all alone. Here we stood 2 Police Officers, 4 NY/NY casino security guards, the manager of the Café and the waitress who served her.

Waitress: are you really going to send her to jail?

Manager: Yes! With a bit of a bark behind it as if he were annoyed by the question.

Security: yeah these people come in here a lot and order steaks and stuff and don't pay! He spoke with an authoritarian tone to his voice.

Me: relax man; she obviously has some challenges here. Give me a second and let me see what we can work out ma'am.

Canadian: ok, I'm so sorry; I thought I had more money on my card. I really didn't mean it.

As the investigation proceeds I observe the waitress go to a booth about 2 seats behind our Canadian dine and dasher. She quietly handed the customers at that booth who were observing the whole ordeal some cash. The guy at that booth stood up and walked over and said "excuse me Officers but can I pay for her meal"?

Me: absolutely! If that's what you want to do sir.

Manager: well sir you don't have to do that, if you don't want too. He obviously hadn't realized that his waitress had given the man the money.

Nice Guy: Please I insist.

Security: Can he do that?

Me: yes he can

The manager accepted the payment and proceeded to lecture the

terrified Canadian. She paid no attention to him and jumped up and

gave the nice guy a hug and then walked over to his table and

hugged everyone that he was dinning with. I nodded at the waitress

and said thanks. Security stood there with a look of disgust on their

face. Myself and Officer P escorted the Canadian lady to the front of

the casino. She was staying at the Tropicana and knew how to make

it back. Her shuttle was leaving the next day at 1 in the afternoon. A

potentially terrible situation had been completely avoided due to the

generosity of an unknown named waitress and a stranger who I have

named nice guy.

MURDER RAP

8/10/2012 Today my squad worked 17 hrs but it was time well spent. We solved a murder, got the subject in custody, and found the murder weapon. This was such a senseless murder and a waste of life. The suspect killed a man that he was arguing with outside of a Mini Mart over the suspect not being invited to some shitty house party. The worst part is that he killed him after the argument was over. The victim was walking away and this guy engaged him again and then shot him multiple times.

The witnesses later stated that they were arguing about a party that the victim was having at his apartment. The suspect was ear hustling and being nosy when the victim was inside the mini-mart speaking to another person about this party. The suspect heard him talking about it and invited himself. When the victim told him that he wasn't invited the argument ensued.

Johnson (our suspect) is a new age gang banger who belongs to some new hybrid gang and basically felt that he had to defend some bullshit street code or something. The whole thing was terrible and pointless. Not too uncommon unfortunately.

Johnson has a 1-month-old baby that he held hostage while in the residence refusing to come out and deal with his poor decision-making.

Eventually he gave up and came outside with his hands up shirtless and wearing no pants. He was taken into custody without incident. It's safe to assume he stripped down because he wanted to ensure no one from SWAT shot him or maybe he was trying to make a dramatic exit. We were asked to assist homicide detectives with the searching of the residence. Some of the clothes that he wore when he committed the crime were found in his bedroom and the laundry room. The actual murder weapon was found inside of the barbeque pit in the backyard. It was a poorly manufactured revolver. I couldn't help but to think to myself, that this piece of crap gun really killed a man. (I know, I know, people kill people) The victim was shot in the chest, face, and arm. When we continued our search inside the residence, we found two raps that the subject had written. One of them read, "Piss me off and ill shoot you in the face". I'll call that one a clue. You can't make this stuff up. He actually sat down and put that crap on paper.

Prior to us, searching the house the subject's mother only had this to say to us, "please don't mess my house up". It was almost as if she had been in this situation before. Of course, the house was already in disarray. There were clothes thrown everywhere, the poor dog that was inside was terrified, and the kitchen reminded me of a looted convenient store. Nothing in its proper place, filthy dishes loaded on top of the counter and expired food thrown all over the place. I will say this; at least the mother's room was an organized pile of mess.

Sadly this isn't the first nor will it be the last senseless murder that officers will investigate in the Las Vegas valley. There was the homeless gentleman that was found dead by a couple of kids in an open field. His face was smashed in with a boulder. It turns out he was murdered over a box of Popeye's chicken that he grabbed from a guy's car while he was shopping. The guy got so upset over the stolen chicken that he found the homeless gentleman, confronted him, and after beating him up with his bare hands he decided that he

REALLY needed to pay for his crimes so he crushed his skull with the boulder before leaving him there to bleed to death.

Then there's the guy that climbed through his neighbors window and beat him over the head with a toilet lid because he was too noisy. First he beat the man with a wooden guitar but that wasn't doing the job so he stepped it up a notch and used the toilet lid. Some murders are more gruesome then others and leave you wondering why or how could this have happened. Here are a few examples of those murders that leave you questioning humanity.

- The baby that was brutally killed with a hatchet in the middle of the day by a guy that was clearly on narcotics.
- The 10 year old that was choked to death by his 22 year old babysitter with a sock. The 22 year old was later found praying in front of the Luxor (Pyramid) and believed to be schizophrenic. He later killed a man while in custody.
- The bag full of puppies found under the freeway overpass that appeared to have been beaten to death with some type of blunt object.

- The father that beat his 2 month old daughter to death because she cried too much.
- Hit and Run's (especially of children). If the driver would have stopped and rendered aide or even called for medical assistance maybe the victim would have survived.

We experience the occasional contract kill as well, such as the firefighter who paid a homeless man to murder his estranged wife. Both are now in prison. The father of 4 that worked as a strip club doorman that was shot and beaten to death because he badmouthed his boss. The boss didn't appreciate the disrespect so he paid some goons a few thousand bucks to kill the man, because well…firing him wouldn't be good enough.

This doesn't even touch on the suicides that we experience in this city. At one point we had the highest suicide rate of any other city in the world. Averaging 34.5 per 100,000 people over a one-year period, which is nearly 3 times that of other cities our size. Someone has to handle those cases and conduct the investigations.

The police will typically be dispatched first, evaluate the scene for any signs of suspicious circumstances. We then contact the Coroner's office (who averages 5 to 8 autopsies at a time). They handle the person's remains until a family member claims possession of such items. The autopsy process is a life changing experience. The smell when entering the medical examiner officer can knock you on your ass and literally take your breath away. It takes a special person to do that work. They are in that examining room for hours on end, weighing, measuring, sawing, cutting, and splicing human parts and pieces. I've been there before and seen everything from a gangbanger splattered with holes from a close range shotgun round, a mangled jumper from a freeway overpass, to an infant who died during the birth process under suspicious medical circumstances. It's a wild place! The examiners discuss little Johnny's soccer competition, lunch, and anniversary arrangements all while conducting their day-to-day operations. Removing one's brains and other organs or trying to preserve the smallest piece of evidence and preserve it for detectives. God bless them and that line of work. It really is a unique profession that requires nerves of solid steel.

JUST A NOTE

8/18/2012 9-felony pc arrest and 4-misdemeanor arrest. Today was a very successful operation for (SEAC PSU) southeast area command problem solving unit. Some days are definitely more productive than others. Every day that we put on our uniforms and badges we know that we are stepping into an unknown. We have our inside jokes and we play around with one another, but deep down inside our only wish is that each of us goes home at night in the same condition that we arrived. Catching bad guys doing bad stuff is always fun and sometimes exciting but that never outweighs our safety. We care for each and look after one another. None of us want to ever have to inform one of our buddies wives or families that something bad has happened to them.

We enjoy our achievements and celebrate when we have successful operations and stop bad people from doing bad things to good people. It feels great and very rewarding. It's not always full speed ahead. We have our down days and spend some time doing work-ups and planning future operations. Seeing those plans come to fruition is cool and enjoyable but the friendships and the camaraderie that we experience means so much more at the end of the day.

It's a bond that cannot be broken. The folks that you work with become more then friends. They become an extension of yourself and you treat them like family. You find yourself attending parties, weddings, and each other events. When you run into each other in public places outside of work you inevitably end up discussing police related stuff. The job becomes a part of your personality and the people that you meet in the job become a part of your life.

JUST ANOTHER DAY AT THE OFFICE

10/7/2013 Policing can be absolutely amazing and it can be just flat out weird at the same time. Today an elderly gentleman who was born in the 20s had a heart attack while he was driving. He drove his vehicle over the curve and into the bushes then passed away at the hospital. Then I stop a prostitute who was walking home from "work". She has a 6-year-old daughter at home that her aunt babysits for her. The aunt knows exactly what it is that she does and she says that she prostitutes because she never graduated high school, never got her GED and, it's the only way she knows how to feed her daughter.

After that, I stopped a Plymouth Voyager; it looked like it was occupied a couple times, had no registration, no license plates or anything. An asthmatic male was driving it with all his kids in the car, six in total. He was driving all the kids to school. The man had expired insurance but I just couldn't find it in me to write him tickets, so I told him make sure he takes care of it today or as soon as possible. Writing him a ticket would obviously put him and his family into a worse financial situation then he was already in. He knew he was wrong and I could tell that it hurt his pride to be in that situation. It was difficult for him to even make eye contact with me.

Also, in the same neighborhood, we had 2 kids run from an apartment they were breaking into. When we caught them, they said they knew the old lady that lives there would be at church. Two of the four kids had guns on them and their intention was to bum rush her if she was home and steal all of her stuff. Luckily she was not home she was actually at the hospital to check herself in. It's just frustrating that these kids continue to break into people's homes with no regard for anyone's safety, personal property, and the fact that they are carrying guns is absolutely ridiculous.

The kids will tell you I'm going to get a slap on the wrist and I'll be back out. In fact, the new thing for them to do is brag about their weekend thievery at school like its cool and then exchange information on where to find easy houses to break into. Now if a homeowner shoots and kills a kid that's breaking into the house because they're in fear for their life, or protecting their property or whatever it may be, the community will be up in arms and will blame the police department for not doing enough. They will say that the kids were innocent kids and that the homeowner with a gun was trigger happy or some type of a raving lunatic it truly is unfortunate when this can be resolved if the community did a better job of having some type of corrective measures. Unfortunately, some kid's parents support them running around stealing things. The most shocking excuse I ever heard was, I can't afford to buy him nice things so I let him steal, so he can have the things he wants. This is what a mom told me after we arrested little Johnny at least 7 or more times.

Just when I thought that my day couldn't get any weirder I ran into a guy whose moniker is Jesus Christ. That's correct Jesus Christ, he must have been given that name on a previous arrest and an Officer put in on his paperwork. This dude refused to answer to any other name. So I entertained him for a while before letting him go with a warning. After all I wouldn't want to be the guy that writes Jesus a citation for Jay-Walking.

CHRISTMAS DAY LADY OF THE NIGHT

12-25-2013 An older guy driving a White Buick with Florida plates flagged one of my partners J W down. The old guy proceeds to tell her that he needs assistance removing someone from his trailer. Naturally, she calls for another unit and I was the lucky one to get dispatched. The older "gentlemen" then explains that he let a lady of the night (nice term for prostitute) stay at his trailer while he's out of town because he's trying to "help" her out. Well this lady friend who I will call Kim invited someone else to the party and the older gentlemen didn't like that very much. He tells us that Kim invited her brother into the house who just got released from prison and that he's scared of him and wants us to drag him out of the house. Being the skeptic that I am we, drive to the residence but the entire time I do not believe a word of this guy's story.

Once we get to the trailer we enter and the old guy points us to a room and says they're in there. When we open the door a lady in her mid-40s wearing entirely too much makeup rolls over with her twins popping out of her shirt that's clearly too small. We say hey Kim parties over wheres your "brother". Her response was what brother...

oh he left. Being the cunning officers that we are we find the "brother" hiding on the side of the bed curled up in a blanket pretending to be asleep. We awaken sleeping beauty and insist that they get dressed, step outside, and have a conversation with us. After talking to them both for a while I get the true truth.

Old guy picked Kim up while she was prostituting about a month ago. He thought she was so nice that after she rendered her services he offered to buy her lunch. One thing lead to another and the next thing you know she's living with him inside of his vacation home....which is this sleek pimped out trailer equipped with shag carpet, dusty drapes, a blow up mattress and a brand new microwave. Well Ms. Kim felt so comfortable that she invited her "brother" aka her long term boyfriend aka her pimp. The brother proceeds to tell me how nasty the old man is and exactly what kind of sexual favors he's been requesting in exchange for rent!!! All UN protected of course because after all he's older and enjoys the natural stuff. After hearing all of this, I kindly asked the old man to join the conversation. I chewed his ass for flagging down a cop on Christmas and asking us to kick his personal prostitute out of his sex layer...I told him how heartless I though he was and he replied with " well there's no bigger fool then an old man".... to which I replied no bigger fool then a lonely man wrap it up pops. We trespassed the lady of the night and her brother who both left voluntarily and told the old man to choose better company.

REST EASY WARRIORS

06-08-2014 Today was definitely one of the saddest days I've experienced while being a police officer. We lost two of our brothers to a couple of savage maniacs, a self-proclaimed sovereign citizen and his wacked out girlfriend. They ambushed our officers while they were eating chow. Police Officer Igor Soldo and Police Officer Alyn Beck tragically lost their lives in one of the most defenseless ways possible. They never had an opportunity to fight back, to look their enemy in the eyes while engaging them in combat. Their wives are without husbands, and their children are without fathers. The community lost protectors, servants, and heroes.

Officers Soldo and Beck were eating lunch at a small dine in pizza restaurant. Some officers like to eat in public places and stay as visible as possible. It's a way of staying connected to the community. You may be on small break but you are never off. On this particular day, the two individuals who's name I will not reward with a mention in my memoir, went on a search for a Police Officer to murder. In their twisted minds the motive was to kill an officer thus sending some kind of a sick message to the rest of us that we aren't ready for the new revolution or something nonsensical like that.

They walked for hours in search of easy prey. Passing Officers that were gassing their vehicles and conducting other forms of business. Their original plan was to attack an Officer while getting gas in his or her patrol car. For whatever reason that plan changed and they carried their selves several miles with duffle bags stuffed with firearms and ammunition. When they came across our officers eating lunch they figured that was just as good a place to commit a ruthless murder as a gas station.

Hearing the details of the call as they came out was crippling. Officers were immediately headed to the scene in hopes of finding a false alarm. Instead they came across our slain brothers and panicked citizens directing them towards Walmart, which is where our suspects had fled. It was the worst-case scenario. Not only did they just execute our brothers but also they are now headed into one of the busiest stores in the area still fully armed and capable of causing much more damage.

Everyone wanted to see this end well. Firearms dropped, hands thrust high in the air, and let the surrendering begin. The word spread quick that our officers were presumed deceased. That news struck like a baseball bat to the chest. As it became clear to us that this was a deliberate attack and that the assailants had no intentions of giving up. Every officer wanted to be there to help facilitate an end to this nightmare. The brave first responders on this call reacted with textbook precision and heroism that would later become doctrine. I commend and respect them for the actions they took on that day. This is a day that will forever haunt our agency and affect the Officers involved negatively.

This incident, which gained national attention, changed the lives of a lot of people. Some emerged as heroes, others realized just how much we mean to one another. The brotherly bond that is built through our experiences helped us all cope. We were still pissed off about the entire fatuous act, but we learned that we are much more enduring than any of us could have ever imagined. Two more funerals and two more families torn apart, these were the good guys both compassionate and bold. They loved the job and anyone that had an opportunity to work with them would tell you how much they enjoyed solving problems and genuinely helping others.

06-12-2014 I've been trying to hide my tears amongst sweat. I figured it's better to train through the pain then show emotion. Well today, the emotions busted through this make believe rough exterior. My heart is heavy. The fallen are to be mourned but not to the extent, that it eats you alive. I honestly feel like I'm falling apart. The senseless death of two patriots and community servants cut me deep, hell it cut an entire community deep.

People that would never look at me in the past are now stopping to say thank you and offer their condolences. Flat out, this sucks. Families without their sons and all because of some nonsensical ideology, Igor Soldo and Alen Beck did not deserve the vengeance that was brought upon them. They didn't deserve the anger that was delivered to them, and damn sure didn't deserve to die a defenseless death at the hands of two cowards. I'm angry, and sad. In fact, I'm angry because I'm sad. No one deserves this hurt. Not even the families of the two lunatics responsible for their deaths. No one deserves the heavy burden of wondering why this materialized.

There are a few officers that I know that have had to take some time off. I get it! We all grieve differently, we all handle extreme stress in our own way. Heck some of us don't handle or can't handle it. I have heard rumors of officers seeking counseling after tragic events. But it's always rumors. No one will ever come forward and say YES this bothers me. I need help and I need it now. Instead we deal with it. That's a dangerous thing to have happen inside of anyone's mind, especially those that are frequently exposed to such tragedies. Dealing with one death and then being hit with another is hard on the soul. Insert any tragic event it doesn't have to be a death and that bears down hard and heavy on you as a person. I commend those that have the guts to speak out about it. I'm not that strong. I keep to myself, pretend that it's all good, and keep showing up and doing my job.

Separating the events as moments in time trying to never allow them to connect. Imagine glitter on a blank sheet of paper. No rhyme or reason behind the placement of the dots just harum-scarum. An explosion of lawless glitter on a sheet of paper, now imagine that sheet of paper is a Police Officers heart, soul, mind or wellbeing. The dots are events; spaces in time that just occur and land where they land. We don't draw lines and try to connect those dots. That would just add to the muddle. Instead we shake that sheet of paper off and hope that the large clunks of lawless glitter fall off. Some remnants may remain, but that's still better than the entire botched mess wasting away in your mind.

This shaking off process happens in so many different ways for folks, oscillation, bumping, or tossing. I've seen officers oscillate by rotating bureaus and trying to change the color of the glitter so to speak. Some bump, by staying in place but changing shifts. Maybe if I see the same faces during the daylight hours instead of at night things will be different. Tossing can be a literal form of a dull fledged adult temper tantrum. I'll just toss my worries away by acting out of character, drinking more, being involved in riskier activities, TOSSING and turning at night. It's a real struggle that is often dealt with through avoidance or denial. I just don't sleep well at night, I need a vacation, and geez I keep getting these headaches. Yet most of us consider it weak to ask for help.

NEW AREA NEW ME

09-28-2014 It's been an interesting couple of weeks. I got moved from Southeast area command to South Central area command. My shift got changed and so did my days off. Initially I was upset about the move. Shift work is already hard enough. When you have to make changes like this it throws your entire family dynamic off. I had worked at southeast for over 7 years and felt comfortable with the area. Comfort in police work is definitely not a good thing. Comfort equals complacency and complacency is a killer.

The move has been productive for me. I have found my rhythm again and enjoy doing my job. Showing up to work doesn't seem like a chore anymore. It's not that I wasn't happy at my other area command; it's just that I developed a routine. Its human nature, you don't intend on falling into a routine it's just something that happens.

The department has been dealing with a broken radio system for a few years now. It finally became bad enough that the Sheriff ordered all personnel to ride as two man units. The radio has suffered total catastrophic failure on multiple occasions, which has resulted in the loss of life at least once and the potential loss of life on a few other occasions. It really is a tragic situation. Since moving over to South Central area command, I have been riding with Officer Mars. Mars is a chiseled young officer that is in amazing physical shape. He almost resembles the box shape of a model in a fitness magazine. He's a loud dude from somewhere in New York. Buffalo I believe. Mars and I are complete shit magnets. We have had the worst cases in our short tenor in South Central together. We have caught 2 murderers, several violent offenders, saved a handful of kids from their abusers, and under complicated some of the shittiest cases I think I have ever handled since jumping into this profession. Times have been good at work. All of this good policing helps the time go by fast.

JAIL

11-6-2016 Our department is shorthanded in a major way (as are many across the country). They have opened up the jail for Patrol Officers to back fill Corrections. I was working at the jail yesterday and saw some pretty interesting stuff that I thought was noteworthy. Granted the jail is full of folks that are probably experiencing one of the lowest points in their life. For some it's just another weekend. The Clark county jail definitely has its fair share of regulars, which is a whole other topic that I could speak about for hours. I would like to share with you 3 characters from my Sunday jail experience.

First we have Mr. John Doe. This guy is awesome from a stubborn citizen standpoint and a giant pain in the ass as far as law enforcement is concerned. Apparently he was stopped by a couple of officers as a result of a loitering call for service. He refused to leave and also refused to identify himself so that he can be cited for trespassing (on a WARNING citation). The officers were then forced to bring him to the jail to try to identify him via fingerprints and such. Needless to say that failed as well. He had heavily damaged hands. I kindly explained the process to Mr. John Doe and his quick-witted reply was this… "Huh I watch the first 48 I'm not saying nothing"!!! My immediate response was "really"! I just explained to you that if you sign this WARNING you will be released immediately, have no court date, and no fines affiliated with this incident. He stuck to the first 48, I'm not going to talk, tough guy act for my entire 12 hr shift. I checked on him from time to time trying to engage in simple conversation. Mr. Doe "where you from"… his response, "HA, I aint saying nothing"! Mr. Doe "who's your football team"? His response, "come on Hartfield I aint saying nothing". Mr. Doe "you ready to go through the process"? I just need your name real quick to put on this WARNING citation. His response, "Hartfield leave me alone… if you're going to charge me, then charge me". At this point I was convinced that he was crazy.

On my way out for the day, I gave it one more try. Mr. Doe "you sure you want to stay here, let me help you walk through the process". His response, "thank you Mr. Hartfield but you know what it is, you've been the realest dude today, but I'm chillin". Awkward moment nonetheless, I quickly realized that he was quite intelligent and probably just wanted the entertainment and companionship for the day.

The next situation was pretty damn sad. A couple of patrol guys were escorting this handcuffed elderly gentleman into the jail facility. He had a nice white suit that was heavily splattered with blood. I asked the gentlemen if he was ok and he immediately began to explain his story in a very soft spoken and fragile tone. "What's my bail amount Mister I want to call my niece and have her bail me out of this joint, I did nothing wrong". His head filled with staples and lumps. Now my interest is peaked. I asked one of the officers what brought them in today. Officer Johnson states that Mr. Peabody stabbed his wife after church and his wife hit him over the head with a glass lamp to get him to stop assaulting her. WELL that's definitely not what I was expecting to hear.

I helped to escort Mr. Peabody inside of the jail because he could hardly stand, or walk alone without assistance. I asked him when he was born. "Jan 21st 1933 in ArKANSAS". 83 years young, Mr. Peabody wanted to be feisty but something tells me that his head wounds and his trip to the hospital exhausted him. I continued to search him and placed him into belly chains. He was frail and fragile to say the least. He was still very kind to me in his soft-spoken voice. He tried to explain what occurred that caused his injuries, in his mind at least. He stated that someone had come into his house and attacked him and he wanted justice. He didn't understand why he was being arrested. I asked the Officers about Mr. Peabody's criminal history. He had only been arrested one other time in his life. 1985 for an old traffic warrant for an unpaid speeding citation. This guy went 20 plus years without any kind of police contact and now he's in jail facing a potential attempt murder charge and he's probably suffering from some form of dementia. Terrible situation for everyone involved, but that's the system.

My final situation that I would like to share is for adults only. This one is funny as hell in a weird and twisted way. Let me set the scene for you. There is probably 5 or 6 corrections officer sitting in the booking area at any given time. Between processing folks and checking side cells we kind of sit around and shoot the shit a bit. While were hanging out a Patrol officer pulls up to the front of the property and frantically asked for help. He has an unruly female in the back of his vehicle that he can't control. We all get up and go to help the officer. The female is handcuffed and screaming at the top of her lungs in an extremely provocative voice (with a heavy Spanish accent) "Ouch take it out it hurts, take it out your hurting me". Were all puzzled by her words! One of the female corrections officers asks the lady what hurts and she shouts, "Everything, you're hurting me". Mind you at this time only 2 officers are even touching this lady and they are simply holding her arms with a light grip trying to prevent her from falling forward back into the patrol vehicle. Once she's out completely she goes silent.

The female Officers continue to search her prior to escorting her into the facility and she belts out loudly "Ay dios mio" with her thick accent. It went from completely silence to that… I chuckled slightly because I thought it was funny. As did the other officers standing around. She was so loud that the Sergeant came out of the facility to check on the situation. The lady failed to comply and separate her feet so she could be searched. The officers asked her kindly again and she refused so they moved her feet for her. She again shouts, "Take it out take it out". Everyone kind of looks around at one another like…take what out.

This lady is a bit heavy set and is wearing a tight form fitted black dress. It looks like she was out at a dinner party or some other formal engagement. She has a belly on her so it's hard to tell if she is pregnant or maybe just heavy set. We ask her if she's pregnant (a reasonable question given the circumstances). She snaps her head to the side and calmly says take it out you're hurting me. One of the officers ask her in Spanish if she is pregnant and again she says take it out you're hurting me. At this point I'm thinking that these are the only English words that she knows.

She's refusing to walk, so she gets a little extra push by the officers into the search area. She's screaming provocatively the entire time.

Once they get her into the search area she tries to bite one of the officers so they grab her hair and turn head away from everyone. As soon as her hair was grabbed the situation got a little bit more awkward. The officer that pulled her hair to hold her head away from officers was standing behind her but bladed off to the side. The lady shouts one more time take it out you're hurting me and then proceed to make it rain from her vaginal area. She begins to pee all over the 3 officers that are dealing with her. She then let's out a sigh and doesn't say another word the entire time. She came in, got her hair pulled, pissed all over a bunch of CO's, and immediately felt relieved. I walked over and found a few orderlies and asked them if they could clean up the mess. She was placed in a side cell and we never heard a peep out of her again.

3-27-2017 Adult Daycare is the process of maintaining accountability of multiple adults with various mental, medical, and social disorders, criminals or at least folks that were in the midst of dealing with the criminal justice process. JAIL is not a fun place; there is nothing appeasing about being locked indoors with others for days, months, or years on end. It's always freezing inside of the jail and cool 42 degrees to help combat bed bugs and other creepy crawlies. Several of the tiers are overflowing so they place about 20 cots on the ground with a paper-thin mattress on top. The inmates receive a small blanket and sheet set to cover the mattress, which is wrapped in plastic. You must ask for everything in jail.

- C.O. can I have soap (they commonly refer to them as tic-tacs because they resemble the tiny, minty breath freshener).
- I need pads please (the women are restricted to 3 a day as some attempt to flood the tiers with excessive pad flushing).
- Can I go to the bathroom?
- Do we get free time today (during free time they are allowed to watch limited television, exchange books, and make telephone calls)?
- Can I send my lawyer a kite (a kite is a jailhouse term for message or note)?
- When is commissary being delivered?
- I need the nurse.

It's nonstop, especially in the female tiers. They tend to be much needier. The propensity for violence or total chaos to erupt at any time is always at a peak. Normal is not an acceptable ambience within the walls of inmate housing facilities.

Tough, troubled, mentally incapable of accepting society's rules and regulations, that's how most choose to be viewed. The harder you appear the lower your chances of being messed with seem to be. Unless of course you have the unpleasant experience of running into another one of society's miscreants that you had some beef with on the outside. Excuses are plentiful, stories are vibrant, and the bullshit bounces off the walls like a game of racket ball.

- I took the charge for the big homies.

- My public defender didn't listen to me.

- The cops messed up.

- I'm waiting to get bailed out.

- They never read me my rights (one jail house lawyer professed).

- It's because I'm off my meds.

- They slap you then go to court on you (as one prostitute explained to another about her pimp testifying against her in court earlier in the day).

- The only reason they caught me was because of _____ fill in the blank.

After a while all of the excuses start to grind together like a vomit smoothie inside of a blender of concocted societal bowel movements. It's a lovely stench. You would think that one solid whiff of this stench would be enough to force a person to NEVER want to return. The madness of jail is confusing and withdrawn from the rest of the world. That confusion may be the exact thing that brings some frequent flyers back. Through the confusion lays a certain amount of order. The kind of quasi-militaristic order that some of them yearned for as young adults, the basics, nothing too out of the ordinary, boundaries, a steady schedule, and the enforcement of simple manners (please and thank you). I've noticed that some folks actually thrive in jail. The very folks that seem to not be able to get function one bit in the outside world do exceptionally well in this ordered, mandated, locked down environment. I'm not sure if it has anything to do with being able to keep them from their own destructive vices or the fact that they are just better at following orders then making their own decisions.

I often find myself wondering how they would have done in the actual military. Would they have survived the rigors of training and met the disciplinary requirements? Some of these folks are veterans. Some of them have served their country honorably and then something went wrong at some point in their lives or they simply found themselves in the wrong place at the wrong time.

Either way it leads one to wonder why anyone would wait until they're in this environment to decide to get their act together. Not all folks that land themselves behind these cold concrete walls straighten up while in custody. For some the show must go on and being put into custody is simply the introduction. For some frequent flyers it's the intermission. Special circumstance inmates can prove to be an obstacle all their own, everything ranging from the mentally ill, sexual deviants, violent seekers, to the everyday drama queens. It's all here, one giant pot of Jail Gumbo. Seasoned as salty as they come.

Speaking to a corrections officer and asking them what are some of the craziest things you've ever seen is like watching an episode of the twilight zone. Be prepared to follow them down that dark and twisted rabbit's hole. Most are so cynical they actually enjoy telling the stories and will do so with a straight face that seems to lack any signs of emotions; Their beady eyes looking everywhere but into your eyes as they tell their horror stories in plain language with little to no flair, as none are really needed to get the point across. In speaking to one corrections officer I can recall him telling me the story of a male inmate that shoved a small pencil up the shaft of his penis.

Me: "Why"? As I looked at him explaining the story I realized what a silly question that was.

Corrections Officer: Because the voices inside his head keep telling him to.

He further elaborated. I was walking the tier and knew something was wrong with fuck stick because he was curled up in the corner during free time. I nudged him and he just groaned as he lay there in agony. The other weirdo's in the tier knew exactly what had happened because he kept yelling his plans at himself out loud while he was locked inside of his room. I'm going to do it, I'm going to fucking do it, just stop pushing me. I rolled him over and saw blood all over the front of his blues. I thought he ripped his sin stick off but nope. He shoved that damn pencil right up there. So far that the infirmary couldn't just push the damn thing back out. Being the C.O. on duty for that tier I was lucky enough to accompany him to the hospital. The good doctors at the county hospital emergency room knew our buddy all too well. They were doing training rotations with Residents. One of the Residents asked if they could take a look at the mess under the blanket. He looked at the bleeding, swollen penis and laughed. Another resident in the group recognized our buddy because he had removed a pencil from his penis a few weeks prior. You mind the resident asked? Go for it! He began to push the pencil back out of the shaft and it appeared to be moving along finely. Then all of a sudden half popped out and the other half lay lodged broken inside of this dudes penis. Surgery! Yep you guessed it surgery said the doc. They called in an urologist and you guessed it I got to hangout during that process. They put fuck sticks legs up on stirrups and then gassed him out. Then they shoved this giant metal thing down his shaft and when they pulled it out the rest of the pencil was out, just like that. When he woke up, he felt every bit of that shit. It was kinda cool. But I got one better than that.

Me: What could be better than a pencil dick?

Corrections Officer: Ass man!

He said it with such conviction I had to get the details. It's not that I really wanted to know the intimate details about a man and his ass but I wanted to know how he earned the nickname "ass man".

Correction Officer: Pretty simple he shoves his hand up his ass, so we call him ass man.

Me: That simple huh?

Corrections Officer: Yep that simple. He was raped as a kid by one of his uncles or something like that and now he shoves his hand up his ass. So when he's in here we make him wear these giant mittens. Its saves us a trip to the E.R. with another inmate with a bloody ass.

Me: Another? I was puzzled by the *"another"* part of his speech

Corrections Officer: Yeah sometimes a bigger inmate will get a hold of a weaker inmate and well you know what these guys do to each other. But that's nothing compared to the females. Those chicks are total savages.

Me: Yeah I can only imagine, every time I have worked at the jail the females give me the most uneasy feeling. They just seem less stable.

Corrections Officer: They are emotional, violent, and over react to almost everything. I have seen chicks slash other chick's faces over phone usage, commissary, and hell even sanitary napkins. Those bitches are flat out mean. Don't look'em in the eyes either. It's a trap. They try to win you over with that girl charm. That shit will get you stabbed by one of these chola's or the psycho white girls. The black chicks like to scrap. Straight up with their fist, they will beat a C.O. down with the quickness.

Me: Note taken!

The callousness of it all seems so sure real. But it's not, this is real life, these are real people. True emotional beings, with zero respect for the concept of life and the concept of happy endings. The inmates were never the worst part of the jail experience for me. It was the twisted folks responsible for babysitting inside of adult daycare. These were the ones that always struck me as odd. We work for the same agency yet they chose to spend their time tucked away indoors for 12 hours at a time watching over people. When I started picking up extra shifts at the jail I had no idea what to expect. In the streets, patrol officers have this unwritten rule that no matter how you feel about a guy/gal they are your brother/sister and you always have their back. Regardless of the situation, race, age, gender if they are in need you do what you can to get to them and help. I'm not saying that corrections officers don't want to jump in and do what is needed for their fellow officer. These guys and gals are professionals and take the job serious. There is no clearer example of this camaraderie then in the central booking area.

The break room or the dining facility is where you can see a clear divide amongst the officers that work inside these doors. As soon as you walk into this area you can physically see the barriers that have been built between the various groups of employees. The Filipino nurses all hover into one corner and eat their salads while speaking Tagalog and snickering at every female officer that enters the room. The white males with their crew cut hairstyles and seasoned look of despair on their faces. They congregate near the coffee machine each clutching their own mugs as if their paychecks depended on it. Next, you have the black corrections officers these guys have a swagger all their own. Half of them are unshaven (shaving profile I'm assuming) and feature a common fade style haircut that has waves on the top, and a low shave in the back and sides. They laugh loudly, together, it's almost in unison talking about games, kids, and concerts, whatever the random conversation of the hour may bring. But these dudes will crack a joke and laugh about anything in the room and not care about who's watching or what their perception may be.

The Latin officers, Mexican, Dominican, and Puerto Rican all together watching something of Hispanic origin on the television mounted on the wall. If everyone exited the room at once and a single soul entered they could point out instantly where each ethnic group was sitting by what was playing on the televisions. Maybe that's why so many are mounted to the walls in the cafeteria? Some of the groups get separated into sub-groups. Young officers or rookies and the more seasoned officers we call SALTY. The salty old dogs are usually striking up a conversation about retirement plans, or their next big vacation. Often times you can overhear the occasional conversation about a pending divorce. "Yeah this is number 2 for me". "2 HA! I'm on my third and I really messed up this time, we bought a house together. What the hell was I thinking"?

While eating a salad in the break area and alternating my caffeine drinks between Mountain Dew and Coffee one evening at around 2 A.M. I overheard a conversation that I hope I never have. A SALTY old C.O. was "schooling" a rookie. Not on the ends and outs of use of force reporting or how to milk the system for overtime without being jacked on your taxes. NOPE! This conversation was about something that was so much more important than any of those topics. He was trying to talk the poor kid out of getting married.

SALTY C.O.: So rumor has it you set a date.

Rookie: Yeah man, were going to one of the Islands near Hawaii next summer.

SALTY C.O.: Sounds expensive. How much is that whole thing gonna run you?

Rookie: Were still working out all the numbers and stuff, that's why I'm killing the O.T. right now. I wonna make sure I'm prepared you know?

SALTY C.O.: Oh yeah I know exactly what you're saying. Prepared to give up half! You ready for that kid? You ready for that look in her eyes in the court room when she's taking you for everything you got. Does she work?

Rookie: Not yet, she's finishing up school.

SALTY C.O.: Ha "finishing" up school. I bet she never graduates. Just wait, you'll see she will come in all fat and pregnant one day telling you she can't finish and then refusing to work. Then you'll need the overtime just to keep up with her habits and your truck payment. You'll see, just watch. It never fails. Hey John-John. The SALTY Dog called out to another older gentlemen in the room. He was sitting at one of the black tables. "What's up man", he answered. Tell the rook about marriage.

John-John: Don't do it! I'm on divorce number 2 and baby number 3, I aint never retiring man. As soon as I do my ex-wives get to collect. Imma work in this place until I drop.

SALTY C.O.: How long you been on now John-John?

John-John: 24 and half long ones buddy, with nothing to show for it.

I listened on as they laughed about how bad they had it. The rookie seemed un-phased by their bitter discontent towards his marriage plans. (I secretly thought, good for him) He just sat there and listened. He didn't offer any rebuttals. It was as if he had been down this road before. Heard this conversation before. It was nothing new, another group of deranged senior officers trying to take him away from his future wife. He knew that his heart was in the right place. I thought the conversation was quite entertaining from a theatrical standpoint. Once the two senior guys got going they never let up. Exchanging horror stories and bad marriage practices with the room. At one point it was as if they were two loan actors on a stage speaking to a crowd of people. They were unbothered by the fact that the rookie was no longer paying them any attention. His mind had drifted elsewhere, probably onto the thought of his bride to be. Randomly John-John and the Salty C.O. would summons someone else into the conversation and get them to share there failed marriage monologue.

The more I listened the sadder the whole thing seemed. Here these guys were, public servants. A couple of men who had dedicated their lives to their community and in the interim lost focus on the things that were important. They became slaves to the money and the system. Overtime whores as we like to call them. They would take a 12 hour shift on their kid's birthday because after all they "needed" the money. They would stay over after working their regular shift even if it were their anniversary because hanging with the fellas was easier to deal with plus they got paid time and half. Not a bad wage for a fair days work. Besides (as most of them would protest) their old ladies wanted the check more than they wanted them around. Absolutely not true at all in most cases but this is the façade they had created over the years and it made it easier to cope with rather than deal with the fact that their job and its stress is what was causing the divide in their families. I just sat there and listened to this madness and thought damn, it's a twisted world. If these guys weren't discussing there failed marriages they were talking about their last drunken concert or some hobby they just spent a small fortune on for the weekend. It was actually quite pitiful in the end. I sat there and offered no guidance to the rookie, and didn't dare interrupt the senior officers and their escapades. I just left it alone, alternated by caffeinated beverages, and then went back to my assigned tier to continue my duties of providing over watch at adult daycare.

WHO KNEW

When I started logging life events I never knew it would turn into a book or a memoir. It started as a logbook in Iraq, and then progressed as an outlet for the many things pinging around in my head. Who knew that someday I would be holding a printed copy of my thoughts? Who knew that anyone would read it or that it could feel this good to complete this process? I have lived a pretty amazing life thus far and can only pray for many more days of adventures and future stories. Writing has not occurred as often as in the past but I still have tons of material. Maybe one-day Ill commit to a second project and write about my military career and experiences. My military memoirs and memories may bring someone peace of mind or perspective into the madness in a military persons mind before, during, and after service. Perhaps someone reading this can relate to my story or it helps one reader understand the rigors of policing and possibly changes their perception. Maybe none of that happens and a few people get a good laugh from the stories listed. Either way I can say that this journey has been interesting and certainly one to remember. It may not be a popular profession but it certainly is one that is needed. Regardless of what walk of life you are from the police can have an impact on your life. Some experiences are positive some are negative by the sheer nature of our profession. Through a continued push of community based policing and mentoring programs it is my hope that we can continue to proactively deal with Americas policing quandary together. Not all citizens are out to commit crimes, just as not all Cops are bad Cops. Exposing the poorly trained or ill willed officers should be just as large of a priority as educating the community. The sheep dog shall protect the sheep from the wolves until the wolves become the weak and weary. The sheep may then peacefully enjoy the pastures as the sheep dog play in the fields while willingly watching their six.

To the WORLD you may be but ONE person,

but to ONE person you may be the WORLD

Made in the USA
Lexington, KY
30 October 2017